## FATHER HAMMOND WAS WALKING BEHIND THE FENCE NEAR MIDNIGHT WHEN HE HEARD A CLATTERING IN THE CHURCH . . .

The clergyman had come to Boston three years ago, in 1960, from a small church in the country. John F. Kennedy had worshipped here several times, and Father Hammond had heard the President's confession.

Now a faint glow came through the stained glass, where all had been dark before. Entering, the priest saw that the altar candlestick had been lit. There was a gentle sobbing coming from the confessional. "Hello?" Father Hammond called. There was no answer, but the sobbing continued.

As Father Hammond seated himself on the other side of the booth, prepared to hear confession, the sobbing stopped and the candle went out.

Hours later, awakened by more sounds of sobbing, the clergyman pulled on a robe and hurried to the church. The candle was once again lit and he entered quietly, so as not to disturb his mysterious visitor.

A man was kneeling by the high altar. He wore a suit, the back of which seemed to glisten in the faint light of the candle. He was sobbing, his face in his hand.

The priest approached slowly. When he was only a few paces away, he said, "My son, is there some way I can help you?"

The candle went ou̲ ̲ ̲ ̲ ̲ ̲ ̲ ̲ ̲ ̲ ̲ ̲ n with the shadows. ̲ ̲ ̲ ̲ ̲ ̲ ̲ ̲ ̲ d there staring at th ̲ ̲ ̲ ̲ ̲ ̲ ̲ ̲ ̲ d witnessed a miracl ̲ ̲ ̲

The following day, President John Kennedy was assassinated in Dallas. . . .

# THE SPIRITS OF AMERICA

## JEFF ROVIN

**POCKET BOOKS**

New York   London   Toronto   Sydney   Tokyo   Singapore

An *Original* Publication of POCKET BOOKS

POCKET BOOKS, a division of Simon & Schuster Inc.
1230 Avenue of the Americas, New York, NY 10020

ISBN: 0-671-67787-X

First Pocket Books printing May 1990

10  9  8  7  6  5  4  3  2  1

# Contents

# CONTENTS

## Contents

# Introduction

It's said that the ghost of Christopher Columbus haunts the beaches of Hispaniola.

At first, that would seem to be an odd place for the explorer to be seen; after all, it was on San Salvador that Columbus first landed in 1492. However, as with many ghosts, it is a site of emotional trauma that appears to attract him. It was on Hispaniola that Columbus left behind a complement of men to establish a fort. When he returned on the second of his four voyages, the men were all dead.

Inhabitants of the island say that the griefstricken Columbus is still searching for survivors. Others suggest that he is looking for the gold and jewels and great palaces of Cathay and Cipango that he never found. Some say he floats above the ground, his legs still, drifting with the breeze; others say he walks, slowly, leaving no footprints in the sand. Still others say he just stands, barely visible, his clothing, hair, and flesh a pale gray.

Regardless, all agree on one thing: the ghost does not wish to be disturbed. Whenever anyone works up the courage to approach, the specter vanishes in waves, like smoke caught by the wind.

Columbus died in poverty, not knowing he'd reached a land richer than the one he sought. And while we know that Columbus didn't actually discover the continent—native Americans and Vikings were here first—he opened it up to colonization and allowed our uniquely heterogeneous society to be born. It is a society whose people came from Europe, Africa, Asia; a society whose art, literature, music, and manners are uniquely its own.

So, too, are its ghosts.

In England, demon dogs tend to dominate the ghostly realm. In Eastern Europe, witches and vampires are the favored creatures, while in South America, angry gods still roam the plains and mountains. Australia has its bunyips, Norway its trolls, Ireland its banshees and death-coaches, Russia its giants, and Japan its dragons.

But in America, from the spirit of Aaron Burr to possessed computers, from the restless ghost of actor George Reeves to the lumbering apparition of a tyrannosaurus, from rampaging Indians to cursed bikers to spectral trains, our tales are as eclectic as our heritage.

In this book, you will meet fifty such ghosts. The entries are arranged chronologically, determined by the year in which the most famous encounter (or in some cases the only encounter) occurred. While the names of a few towns or participants have been changed to protect their privacy, all the encounters have been carefully researched. Several of the stories were culled from contemporary magazine and newspaper articles, and from books long out-of-print. Many were related by the participants themselves, or by residents of the towns where the older hauntings took place.

All of them happened as described. And any one of them can happen again.

Of course, some researchers dismiss ghosts as pure fantasy. They say that ghosts are the result of self-hypnosis or are projections—electrical outpourings from the brains of the people who see them.

Yet there are others—those who have felt the cold spots in

a room, seen the hazy shapes, ducked the flying plates, or heard the ghastly sounds—who will never be convinced that ghosts are anything but the bona fide spirits of the dead.

Like Columbus setting out across the uncharted Atlantic, keep an open mind as you read. Like Columbus, you, too, may be greatly surprised by what you find at journey's end.

# 1542: Seven Cities of Ghosts

His name was Rodrigo, and his life is a mystery, save for what little was passed along in accounts of his time.

He was a soldier in the service of Spanish explorer and conquistador Francisco Vásquez de Coronado. He was a young man, enthusiastic, hardy—and afraid.

The hardship and frustration were nearly unbearable. Yet, after two years of searching, Coronado was unwilling to give up. Not when the prize—and the sacrifice—had been so great.

In 1540, the thirty-year-old governor of Mexico had left his comfortable command post to mount an expedition to the north, to find the fabled Seven Cities of Cíbola. He had heard Indians and Spaniards alike tell tales of towering walls of gold, of fields where the precious metal lay like common stone, of garments spun from glistening threads.

To claim such a treasure for Spain would be the crowning achievement of any life.

But the quest begun with such high hopes quickly became fraught with disaster. Heat, disease, hunger, insects, and endless marches through barren plains had produced nothing. The only "cities" they discovered were collections of straw huts. Most of the natives they had brought as bearers had died or deserted; many of the men they'd captured along the way had to be slain as an example to the others.

One party which had broken off from the main expedition went to investigate reports of a valley of gold. Months later, García López de *Cárdenas* returned with reports of a great river and a vast *cañon* . . . but no riches and no gold.

Sitting in his tent one evening, studying charts by torchlight, Coronado called Rodrigo and another man to him. He ordered one of the natives they had enslaved to be brought to him. This was done, and Rodrigo was told to remain in the tent with them.

The native youth was lean and bronzed. He wore a hide about his waist, and a band around his long, black hair. His feet were bare. Coronado walked over to the native and, showing him a chunk of gold, pointed west, sketched the sun in the sand, and lowered his hands to indicate it setting.

He was contemplating a journey farther to the west.

The Indian shook his head. He pointed west, picked up sand, and let it fall through his fingers. He spit in his palm and made a sweeping pass over it with his other hand.

Desert and water. He was telling them that was all they'd find.

Coronado regarded the young man intently. Then, removing an ivory-handled dagger from its scabbard, he pushed it through the Indian's heart.

He left the young man's body where it fell, and had Rodrigo bring other natives in turn. They were unfazed by the corpse, and knew nothing of gold to the west. Coronado ordered the body removed and sat back down.

Rodrigo and the other soldier placed the dead young man beside a creek. They piled rocks on the body, and Rodrigo said a short prayer. Even a heathen deserved that much, he felt.

Rodrigo was one of the men posted on watch that night,

and several times his eyes wandered to the mound of stones a short distance away.

Long after everyone else had gone to sleep, Coronado extinguished the torch in his tent.

Before Rodrigo, over a dozen Indians were tied one to the other at the ankles. They did not sleep, but sat cross-legged on the sand, facing the stream, muttering quietly. Now and then they held their arms up, hands pressed together, faces turned to the star-speckled heavens.

Finally, within moments of each other, the men stopped, lay on their sides, and went to sleep.

Rodrigo walked back to the campfire, where another man sat. They threw a few dry sticks on the blaze, grumbled about the mosquitoes, and then sat silently. After a while, Rodrigo went to the stream to get a drink and wash his tired eyes.

Much to his amazement, he found the mound of rocks in disarray. It was too dark to see if the body was gone, or whether there were any animal tracks. Nor was there time for him to search. No sooner had he discovered the desecration than his fellow sentry yelled. There was a fire.

Rodrigo ran back and saw that the governor's tent was ablaze. His companion had already gone inside but was unable to rouse the sleeping Coronado. Rodrigo joined him, and together they carried him out.

There was a deep cut on his head, where he'd been struck.

The tent and all its contents, including the charts, were destroyed. Coronado remembered nothing of the blow he obviously had received, and was amazed that he had failed to extinguish the torch completely, setting his own tent on fire.

This brush with death was the final blow. Taking it as an omen, the explorer declared that the search was ended, and that they would return to Mexico.

Before they left, however, Rodrigo went back to the mound by the river. The pile was not disturbed at all. He must have imagined that. Yet—

Moving several of the rocks aside, he looked down at the body.

The corpse was white and still. But clutched in its right hand was a long, narrow stone. On its tip: blood. It could well have been the blood of the slain native. However, when they had placed the man here, his hands had been limp and empty.

Rodrigo looked back at the natives. Several of them were staring at him.

There was something in their expressions that he hadn't seen before. Not the pride he was accustomed to, but something tranquil. Content.

And he knew, as they left for home, that there was a mystery in it all—one far greater and more profound than the location of the elusive Seven Cities of Gold.

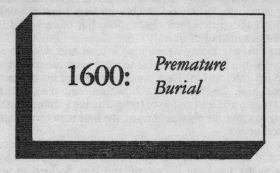

# 1600: *Premature Burial*

Their names have been lost in time; only the event itself survives, passed on as a tale told in the dark.

They were four Montauk braves, and when the aged chief of their tribe died, they were honored with the task of carrying him to his chosen resting place. Traditionally, this was a point well to the east, in the seas off what is presently Montauk Point on the tip of Long Island in New York.

At dawn on the day following his death, the men left their wigwams for the forty-mile trek, carrying the remains of the chief on deerhide stretched between two long poles. Not long after the men set out, however, a winter snowstorm crawled into the region, quickly becoming a blizzard.

Despite the numbing ferocity of the storm, the braves pressed on, their clothes growing wet and stiff. The maize and meat they carried for food was quickly depleted.

After several days, having managed to cover nearly thirty miles, they reached a small rift in the earth. Though this was not where the chief had asked to be buried, it was decided to leave him here. Otherwise, the braves feared that not only wouldn't they reach their destination, but there would be five bodies instead of one.

The rift was nearly as wide as a man and, with some difficulty, the Indians were able to clear away the snow and place the chief within. They pulled the ends of the deerskin around him, covered it with branches, and placed what rocks they could find on top of these. Vowing to return in the spring to move the chief to the sea, the four men turned and headed home.

By nightfall, tired and hungry, they came to a dry, sheltered spot beneath a ledge of rock. The ledge afforded some protection from the storm, and they decided to rest there until the following day.

While two of the braves stalked and captured a wild hare, the other two started a fire. Soon, the men were enjoying a much-needed repast while the winds whistled and the snows swirled.

While their dead chief lay well beyond the greasy gray smoke of their fire, he was never far from their thoughts. They spoke about him; and now that they were dry, and their bellies were full, they began to think about what they had done—how they had dishonored him and shamed themselves. Before lying down to sleep, they decided that the following morning they would return to the rift, disinter him, and continue their journey to the shore.

That night, during the howling of the storm, the men were awakened by a blood-chilling howl. Each brave sat up and looked toward the east, from where the sound had come. It tore through the storm again, followed by rattling, as of a distant landslide.

Fearing that an animal had somehow violated the grave of the chief, the Indians left their shelter, in spite of the knee-deep snows and icy winds.

When they reached the rift, their worst fears were confirmed. The broken earth was empty, the rocks and branches toppled, the deerskin thrown aside. There were prints of some kind in the snow, headed toward the east, but it was impossible to tell whether they were human or animal.

Horrified with the results of their cowardice, the braves

followed the tracks, now and then hearing the same cry they'd heard before. It *could* have been an animal or the wind. But each man secretly believed that it was neither: it was, they knew, the cry of a spirit in torment, a torment for which they were responsible.

The braves travelled until one man fell over from exposure. One man stayed behind with him while the other two went on.

Late the next morning, exhausted and literally crawling through the snow, the braves followed the tracks to a bluff overlooking the ocean. Creeping to the edge and looking down, they saw the chief's body on the rocks below. Waves from the storm-tossed sea slammed ever closer; soon the water enveloped him, and bore his body out to sea.

Just as he had wished.

To this day, the area around the fissure screams with ghostly cries. There are those who attribute the phenomenon to the way the wind passes over the rift. Others insist that it is the sea, which can sometimes be heard as far as twenty miles inland. Some maintain that what the Indians heard that night was the voice of the storm or even of their own consciences. Still others insist that it was an animal which attacked the body, dragged it off, and bayed when it became lost in the storm.

But the braves were convinced that it was the chief they heard, reprimanding them as he took himself to the burial site of his choosing. And many agree, convinced that his spirit lingers still, waiting to chastise those who would leave any job undone.

**1692:** *The Witch's Ghost*

On the morning of the execution, old Colonel Bucks stayed at home.

He closed the shutters, lit a candle, sat in a chair by the cherrywood nightstand, and read from his Bible. It was difficult to concentrate, every small noise distracting him. Shadows moved in the corners of his eyes.

He didn't regret what he'd done, but after a sleepless night, he feared the consequences.

When Salem, Massachusetts, began trying and killing their witches, the tall, distinguished resident of Bucksport, in present-day Maine, listened closely to every traveller who spoke of the hearings. Listened to the reports of animal sacrifices. Of copulation with the devil. Of missing children and hymnals defaced with blood and wells spitting up frogs and rats.

Hearing these tales, Colonel Bucks concluded that witches must be everywhere—even in his own, small town.

With paranoia as his only guide, he kept an eye on the women of Bucksport. Eventually, he singled out a ninety-two-year-old widow, Comfort Aynesworth, a recluse, and began asking about her.

At the local tavern one night, huddled with men hoping to curry the wealthy man's favor, Bucks asked about the woman. The blacksmith said that the wrinkled old woman had several goats and pigs, in which form the devil often walked the earth. He'd also seen her talk to her cat. The town crier suggested that for all they knew, the old woman had killed her husband in an evil rite. The innkeeper added that on still nights, he could hear the woman singing in a strange tongue. It could have been Gaelic, for she was from Ireland, or it could have been backwards-English, the mark of a slave of Satan.

Which was all the colonel needed to hear.

The next day, at a town meeting, Colonel Bucks demanded that the woman be arrested and charged with practicing witchcraft. The order was given, and the old woman was put on trial. As the townspeople sat in smug, self-righteous silence, Comfort's hoarse ranting convinced the judge and jury that she was guilty, and she was sentenced to be hanged. As she was carried from the courtroom, the frantic old woman swung her head back and pinned the colonel with furious eyes.

"Your lies have offended the Almighty! He will help me take your life and leave my mark upon your grave!"

Comfort's blasphemy shocked the courtroom, and as she was led away, screaming oaths, Colonel Bucks resolved to have nothing further to do with the woman, not even to attend her execution. His job was nearly done. All that remained was for him to pray—for her, and for himself.

Now, on the following day, the day Comfort Aynesworth was to be hanged, Colonel Bucks sat in his bedroom, reading from his Bible. The household staff had been told not to disturb him, and he felt very much alone as a late autumn wind blew outside. The trees creaked, shutters rattled, and the dry timbers of his home cracked and popped. He started as, somewhere along the corridor, the wind slammed a door shut.

Bundled in a robe, his feet in old slippers, Colonel Bucks read until the light filtering through the shutters faded. The time of Comfort Aynesworth's execution had come and gone. Her curse—and it *was* a witch's curse, for who else would take the Lord's name in vain?—seemed more tragic than ominous. He didn't understand why she hadn't seized the moment to repent. It wouldn't have altered her fate on earth, but it might have drawn compassion from the God she instead chose to profane.

As darkness settled upon Bucksport, the sounds of the house seemed louder, the rustling of the trees like a great shroud. He felt a sudden chill.

Comfort had said that the Almighty would avenge her. But had she meant his God, or hers?

What did it matter, he asked himself, now that she was dead? Comfort Aynesworth was in perdition, paying for her pact with Mammon, sent there by his own vigilance.

Warmed by the flush of virtue, the colonel set the Bible aside and dressed, intending to ride to town to dine. He also wanted to hear from the blacksmith and the innkeeper and others just how a witch dies.

He wondered, too, if any other women in the village had been acting strangely.

Candle in hand, he walked to the bedroom door. As he turned the knob and opened the door, the flame sputtered and died. Colonel Bucks stood in the doorway, in the thick shadows of twilight, wondering where the breeze could have come from. Had he done it himself, with his own heavy breathing? He heard the floorboards groan and felt another chill.

Setting the candle on a carved oak chest, the colonel went back to the nightstand, plucked a match from a silver ewer, and turned back to the doorway.

And stood stone-still as an icy breeze rushed against him, carrying with it a smell like rotted leaves. He bent forward and squinted down the hallway, for he thought something had moved in the dark.

"Sarah?"

There was a figure walking toward him, but it wasn't the housekeeper. The colonel backed away.

"Who's there? Who is it?"

The intruder did not answer and, reaching behind him, the colonel struck the match on the nightstand. He brought it around, using his hand to shield it from the rank wind. He gazed ahead and gasped.

The newcomer was a woman, and she was approaching sideways.

"Who *is* it?"

As he watched her in the flickering light, he realized that she wasn't walking sideways, but that her head was facing away, turned completely to the left. Her feet were bare and she wore a plain, white dress.

The dress of the hanged.

He began walking back, toward the bed, though his eyes never left the woman. Neither her gown nor her hair moved in the awful breeze, and her feet hardly seemed to touch the floor. Yet she moved quickly, with a speed which somehow wasn't in keeping with her step. It was as though the wind itself were carrying her along.

Transfixed in mounting terror, Colonel Bucks watched as she reached the door and twisted so that her feet were facing to the right—though she continued to move ahead. Colonel Bucks might have been startled by that, had he noticed, but he was staring at her face, which was now upon him. And there was no mistaking who the intruder was: Comfort Aynesworth.

The match trembled in his hand, throwing uneven shadows across the room. The newcomer's head was tilted to one side, the neck bulging on the other, just above a fat blue band which encircled the white flesh. Her eyes were shut, mouth agape, nostrils flared, as though frozen with shock. Her ashen features were made even paler by the deep shadows which lined every wrinkle.

Colonel Bucks tried to speak, but his jaw quaked and the words snagged deep in his throat. He backed against the nightstand, gasping and dropping the match. It burned for a moment on the hardwood floor before dying.

"Please," he managed to croak before his throat froze again. He dragged a hand across his eyes, trying to rub away the apparition. But even in the dark he could feel her presence, could smell the choking odor of death. He looked out again. The figure was just a few feet away now, and Colonel Bucks sat on the nightstand, knocking over the ewer, throwing his arms across his chest in an effort to shield himself.

"Go away!"

The specter's thin arm rose, pointing at Colonel Bucks.

"Come . . . with . . . me . . . ," a woman's voice whispered, though the lips of the specter hadn't moved.

He shook his head violently. The arm lowered from the frightened man to the match.

"Burn . . . and . . . die."

Like a wave, sulphurous heat washed over him, backing the colonel against the wall. His clothes dampened, his mouth burned, his heartbeat quickened. He screamed, shaking and squeezing his eyes shut. Hot tears boiled up behind his lids, forcing them open. When he looked out, the dead face of Comfort Aynesworth was inches from his, the stench of decay causing him to retch.

"Die . . . and . . . I . . . shall . . . be . . . with . . . you. Always."

The colonel barely heard her. Screaming as the heat burned deep inside of him, he fell onto the bed.

Late the following morning, when the housekeeper came to check on him, she found the colonel feverish. He was unable to keep down food or drink, and the physician was summoned. Colonel Bucks was bled, but that failed to break his fever.

The colonel's strength waned quickly, and shortly after dictating a new will, Colonel Bucks died of consumption.

As his new will stipulated, the colonel was buried beneath a tombstone of solid marble, one which could not be marred in any way. Yet on the morning after the funeral, the imprint of a foot was clearly visible on the headstone. None of the abrasives used by the caretaker could remove it. When his family tried to chip it away, the chisel would cut only inside the imprint.

Colonel Bucks's family ordered another marker placed on the grave, but overnight a footprint appeared on that as well.

A third, more expensive tombstone was purchased but it, too, was defaced by the same slender footprint. The colonel's heirs finally gave up trying to fix it.

The defaced headstone stands there still, marked by the woman who wasn't a witch.

Or was she?

# 1743: *Horsing Around*

Frederick Wayne was not a man who took kindly to being robbed.

He was riding home one night from a neighboring farm in Braintree, Massachusetts, when a masked, black-garbed man stepped onto the dirt road in front of him. The stranger held a pair of flintlock holster pistols, both levelled at Frederick.

"I will take your life and your money, or simply your money. The choice is yours."

"I have no money," the fifty-five-year-old replied.

"I know you do," said the other. "I saw you take it from your host in a game. You took his money and his rum. An accommodating guest, you are."

Another masked figure stepped from the woods beside the road, and reached into Wayne's pockets. He pulled out a purse, and also reached for a ring on one of Wayne's thick fingers.

But Wayne, a retired soldier, was not entirely helpless. It was his custom to travel with a dagger up his sleeve, since he had been robbed years before and vowed then that it would never happen again. As the second masked man spit on the ring to get it off, Wayne slowly lowered his other arm, let the dagger slip into his hand, brought it around, and drove it into the man's throat. Simultaneously, he kicked his horse in the ribs and charged the gunman. One flintlock misfired, the shot of the other went wide, and Wayne rode the man down.

The highwayman was bloodied and moaning as Wayne turned his horse around and went back. He dismounted and strode over to the figure, pulling the mask from the man's mouth. He looked down into a scruffy young face.

"You aren't so brash now," Wayne said as he put the point of the blade to the man's chin. "I hope you enjoy the fires of hell, my friend."

With that, Wayne pushed the blade up through the young man's throat. He died gurgling, and, when he was still, Wayne wiped the knife on the grass beside the dirt road. He walked back, and collected his purse. While he was so doing, his horse suddenly reared and ran off. Wayne called after it, but to no avail.

Though he was unhappy at having to walk the rest of the way, he was considerably mollified by the good work he had done. He actually found himself whistling as he walked.

Reaching the farm at around two A.M., he was surprised to find that the horse hadn't come back. Undressing and deciding to send one of his sons out in the morning, he crawled into bed.

Fired by satisfaction over having successfully defended himself, Wayne was unable to sleep. He lay on his back, cherishing the look of surprise on the two men's faces. He was looking forward to telling others what he'd done and hearing their congratulations.

Just as he was finally growing drowsy, Wayne was startled by a clopping sound outside his window.

*The damn horse.*

It had finally come back. Hopefully, it would now have the good sense to go on into its stall.

The hoofbeats stopped. The animal whinnied quietly. Throwing off his quilt, Wayne went to the window and threw it open to shoo the animal along.

But the horse wasn't going to go anywhere. There was a rider on its back: a man dressed in black and wearing a mask. Another masked man stood beside him. A thick band of red appeared on the throat of each man where Wayne had cut them.

The mounted man held a pair of pistols, both pointed at the window. He said in a low monotone, "I'll take your money, sir."

Wayne ran to a mahogany secretary and pulled open the top drawers to get his own pistols. As he loaded them, he shook his head.

He'd killed those men. What was he going to do? Kill them again?

He went back to the window, and sure enough only the horse was there. Too little sleep and too much rum had done him in. Pulling on his breeches and shoes, he went to lead the horse to its stall.

Outside, the men were back as before, waiting for him.

"Your money, sir."

Wayne felt like a fool, standing outside the door half-naked, without his guns or knife.

"It's inside," he said.

"Get it."

Wayne turned and went back inside. What was keeping those two alive? He'd cut their throats. He hurried to his room and loaded his pistols.

The men were still waiting when he went to the window. Without hesitation, he fired once at the man on the horse, then swung the other pistol to the masked figure standing beside him.

The horse bolted and ran. When the smoke cleared, neither man was anywhere to be seen.

Until Wayne turned. He dropped his guns with fright as he saw them standing behind him, their eyes so red that the dark pupils seemed lost in them. The raw slashes in their throats were nearly as dark.

The man with the pistols said, "For the last time, sir, we'll have your money."

Baffled and afraid, Wayne nodded and walked to the secretary. He got his purse and handed it to the bandit.

"Your ring, sir."

He managed to work up enough spit to wet his finger and remove the ring. As he did so, he heard his sons running down the hallway, calling to him. Obviously, they had been awakened by the shots.

Wayne turned to warn them away just as the door flew open. Both young men stood there in their nightshirts; one of them held a candle.

"Get back!"

"Father, what's wrong?"

*"Watch* yourselves!" he yelled, stepping between them— and no one. He looked behind him, then from side to side, and finally out the windows. The intruders were no longer there. "They were here," he said meekly. "Highwaymen, two of them. I slew them on the road . . . and they came back."

Wayne's sons walked over. One of them picked up the guns while the other led his father back to bed.

"You had a dream, Father. A dangerous one—with the pistols and all—but a dream nonetheless."

"No! I tell you, they were here!"

Breaking away from the youths, Wayne ran from the house, pressing on until he reached the spot where he'd killed the highwaymen.

The bodies were gone. He looked in the woods on both sides: there was no trace of them anywhere, nor did he ever see either man again.

Neither did he ever reclaim his purse, ring, or horse.

# 1752: *Headless Nell*

George MacQuillie was sorry he'd let his sixteen-year-old daughter Nell make the trip.

MacQuillie and his wife Virginia owned a small mill on the Pamlico River, near present-day Bath, North Carolina, and Virginia's sister Alice ran a struggling chicken farm fifteen miles away. When Alice broke her leg, there was no one to collect the eggs and to see to other chores, so Nell volunteered to go over every other day to help out. George reluctantly agreed, provided she was home before sunset each day. Though the journey was just fifteen miles, and the cart horse unspirited, the road was rutted from recent flooding and the mud hardened after sundown, making passage on the old cart treacherous.

Now it was after midnight, and when Nell failed to return home, her anxious father took his horse and musket and went looking for her.

George proceeded quickly, the light of the full moon

providing illumination. He called her name every few paces, hoping that if she'd been hurt or thrown from the cart, she'd hear him. The only answer was the droning of the crickets.

As George neared the woods and the pond where he used to take Nell swimming, he stopped; somewhere in the distance he thought he heard the whimpering of a dog.

"Scotty?"

Dismounting and leading the horse behind him, George bent forward slightly and followed the sound.

There was a turn in the road ahead, with woods to the right and a boulder to the left. The whimpering was coming from behind the boulder. Leaving the horse, George hurried ahead.

When the miller reached the boulder, he stopped and looked down. He saw nothing. Walking around it and into the wood, he called the dog's name.

"Scotty!"

Fat clouds had appeared, intermittently blocking the light of the moon. The trees and moss-covered forest floor shifted continuously from blackness to a ghostly blue luminance as he made his way deeper into the wood.

He heard the dog again, this time from over a ridge, near the pool. He ran ahead, and suddenly, the whimpering seemed to be swallowed by the noise of the crickets; a moment later it rose again, further ahead. He followed and it faded, then reappeared nearer to the pond.

George ducked under a wall of Spanish moss and scrambled over the slippery ridge. Finally, after a long period of darkness, the moon came out and the miller saw the cart. It had turned over and was lying nearly on its back beside the pool, one corner in the water. The Scottish terrier was perched on top, its fur matted and dripping. The horse was nowhere to be seen.

With an oath, George ran forward. He tripped over a root, twisting his ankle, and limped painfully ahead, calling his daughter's name.

Nell didn't answer, nor did the dog move.

"Scotty, where *is* she? Take me to Nell!"

The dog was damp but not panting. It just sat, staring down at the miller.

Pulling himself forward on his hurt leg, George went around the cart, and looked down, expecting to find his daughter unconscious.

But she wasn't there. And when George looked back up at the cart, neither was the dog.

He stood in stunned silence for a moment, and then began calling Nell's name. Turning, George was startled to see the dog standing beside the water now. The miller approached, and the terrier backed into the pool, walking beside the submerged corner of the cart, not causing so much as a ripple.

George limped toward the dog, which turned and went under the cart, again without disturbing the water. The miller waded into the pool, shaking now with dread, then stood and waited as a cloud obscured the moonlight.

When pale light once again poured across the pond, George stared down at the body of the dog, which was tangled in the reins of the cart and floating just below the surface. Beyond it, pinned by the corner of the splintered splashboard, was Nell.

*"Noooo!"*

Screaming madly, George charged ahead and tried desperately to move the cart. He managed to work it back slightly, just enough to slide it off.

What he saw then was even worse. Somehow, the cart had turned with sufficient force to push the slab of wood through her neck and sever her head.

Horror overwhelmed George as he stared at his daughter. With the fury of a madman, he pounded his fists against the cart until they were bloody, cursing himself and the cruel God who had allowed this to happen.

"Father?"

The voice was sweetly accented and clear as the moon. The miller spun and saw his daughter standing on the shore, her white cloak glistening with drops of moisture, the hood drawn forward, casting her face in shadow. Scotty sat beside her, as still and as damp as before.

George looked back at the pool. The reins of the cart were floating freely, and there was no body in the silt at the bottom.

It had been his imagination. The shock of seeing the cart overturned.

With a cry of delight, George lumbered to the shore, slowed by boots full of water.

"Father," Nell said again, "Scotty and I were wondering when you would come. Hold me."

His arms outstretched, George struggled ahead while Nell slowly moved her left arm away from her, from inside the voluminous folds of her cloak. As it emerged, he could see her golden tresses, her bright blue eyes, her pretty smile— her head was nestled in the crook of her arm.

George stopped. He saw now that the darkness inside her cowl wasn't shadow—it was emptiness. He stood still, arms still open, paralyzed with shock.

"We kept calling for help," Nell said quietly, "but no one came." She walked into the pool, causing not the slightest disturbance. She put both hands beneath the head and raised it toward him. "Kiss me, Father. Kiss your Nell."

His heart beating in his throat, George saw his daughter slip between his arms just as the moon vanished behind a cloud. When it once again emerged, all was still about the pond, save for the whining of the crickets.

In the morning, Virginia MacQuillie found her husband's horse grazing near the mill. Riding it into the wood, she discovered the cart in the pond, along with the bodies of her daughter, the dog, and her husband—George and Nell entwined, as though he had lain down with her beneath the water and died.

In Bath, those who know of this stretch of woods stay clear of it. For on those nights when the moon is full, a small Scottish terrier can be seen waiting by the boulder beside the road, whimpering. And those who have dared to follow him report having seen Nell at the quiet pool, still calling for help, still cradling her head. Still looking for someone to embrace her.

# 1776: *Wedding Fright*

When word reached General Jonathan Moulton in September of 1776 that the Continental Congress had declared the colonies independent of British rule, nothing could have kept him in Hampton, New Hampshire, not even his new bride.

It had been a summer of profound sadness and joy for the officer. In June, his wife of twenty years, Abigail, had died of pneumonia. Now, two months later, he had taken as his second wife beautiful Sarah, the widow of a young cobbler who had died in the fighting at Concord.

Their wedding night was the first and only night the couple would have together before General Moulton rode north to Portsmouth to join his men.

The small saltbox house was situated on the main street, built by Jonathan and Abigail when they had first married. Sarah felt awkward moving into the home so soon after Abigail's death, but Jonathan had worked hard to put her at ease. Now, early in the evening on their wedding day, when the few guests had left the reception to be home before last light, Sarah went upstairs and sat at the sycamore commode, brushing out her hair.

Looking in the drawers for a hair fastener, she was surprised to find several pieces of fine jewelry in the top drawer.

"I'd been saving those for later," Jonathan said, stepping up behind her and kissing his wife on the neck. "They belonged to Abigail's mother, and Abigail always regretted that she had no daughters to whom to give them. I'm sure she would have wanted you to wear them."

Hesitantly, Sarah selected a silver necklace with a small pearl at the end. Jonathan did up the clasp, and Sarah brought the candle closer and looked at herself in the mirror.

"It's beautiful," she said, smiling, "but I—"

"—Will wear it every day until I return home," Jonathan interrupted. "Will you promise me that?"

Lightly brushing her hand across the necklace, Sarah promised, then hugged her husband.

Jonathan left the next morning at dawn, riding into a storm. One last time, he'd asked Sarah if she wouldn't rather stay with her parents, but she had insisted that this was her home. Lightning lashed the slate-gray skies as Sarah stood in the door waving to her husband, her left hand stroking the necklace. It felt as warm and soft on her throat as the parting kiss Jonathan had given her.

When the general was lost in the morning mist, and she could no longer hear the clomping of the horse's hooves, Sarah shut the door. She lifted the candle from the card table and stood for a long moment, feeling proud, yet worried about the dangerous job Jonathan had ahead of him.

She was still rubbing the necklace when she started upstairs. Lightning erupted overhead, and thunder rocked the house. The silver chain suddenly felt tight, and she stopped rubbing it. She ran her finger round it, between the silver and her neck, felt nothing different. Yet when she stopped, the chain grew tighter, and upon reaching the landing, she looked into the gilded wall mirror.

The pearl hung low as before, the chain was loose again, and nothing was different—save for a slight crimson mark around her throat. She thought she saw something move at her side, but decided it was just smoke from the candle.

Hurrying to the commode, she gently lifted the chain and patted water on her skin. The redness went away, and Sarah sat back, studying the necklace in the small built-in mirror.

As she wondered what had caused her throat to tighten like that, there was a scratching noise in the drawer beside her. Fearing a rat, she went to the bed and brought over a pillow, intending to trap the animal and drop it in the water bucket out back.

Cautiously opening the drawer, Sarah was shocked when Abigail's rings suddenly flew out like buckshot. She jumped back as the rings settled on the floor, near the open door. Trembling, she looked inside the deep drawer to see if an animal had tossed them out. As she brought the candle over and bent to look down, she felt a tug on her throat. The necklace was tightening again, only this time the chain pulled her back, away from the drawer.

Sarah dug her fingers under the constricting necklace, and pulled it from her flesh. The silver chain relaxed again.

"Miiiiine."

The voice was an airy whisper, coming from all around, clearly heard despite the drumming of the rain.

"Who's there?" she asked, looking quickly around the bedroom.

"Miiiine," the voice repeated, as the rest of the jewelry began shaking inside the drawer. A moment later, it flew out and landed beside the rings.

Eyes wide, Sarah gagged as the necklace twisted and pulled her back again, toward the door. She reached for her throat, but this time wasn't able to slip her fingers under the chain. The metal cut into her flesh, drops of blood running onto the frilled collar of her housecoat, and she fell to the floor, gasping for air.

Whether it was pain or dizziness or a trick of the storm, Sarah saw a hazy figure standing above her, a form like smoke from a snuffed candle. Only the shifting shape had a face, a woman's face, with dark holes where the mouth and eyes should have been.

The wide mouth moved.

"Miiine," it uttered once more, as a smoky tendril reached out and turned the chain even tighter.

There was the sound of hoofbeats outside, and a moment later the front door flew open.

*"Sarah!"*

Unable to draw breath, the young woman pulled over the chair beside the commode, and Jonathan came running up. Seeing the deep gash in his wife's throat, he ripped off the necklace and carried Sarah to the bed. He hurriedly filled the basin with water and cleaned her wound.

"I *saw* her," he said breathlessly. "I was passing the cemetery, and I saw Abigail. She was walking toward the house!"

"The jewels," Sarah gasped. "She . . . wanted them."

They both turned, then, to look at the jewelry, which had been scattered about the floor. All of it was gone.

Jonathan remained with his wife until late in the morning, after which he took her to her parents' home by the Piscataqua River.

However, on the way out of Hampton, they stopped at the cemetery; both stood in dead silence as they stared at the grave of the late Abigail Moulton.

The jewelry was all there, the ends of the necklaces drawn into the rain-softened earth, the rings and bracelets half-buried. The couple exchanged a silent look, and turned back just in time to see an opal bracelet sink into the mud.

After that, the general and his new bride never returned to the house or to Hampton. Now that she had what she wanted, neither did Abigail.

**1777:** The Ghost at Valley Forge

*As I was sitting at the table . . . something seemed to disturb me. Looking up, I beheld, standing opposite me, a singularly beautiful female figure. . . .*
—George Washington

During the hard and lonely winter of 1777, George Washington and the soldiers of the Continental Army were encamped in Valley Forge, Pennsylvania, twenty miles from Philadelphia—and its warm, well-fed British captors.

Poorly supplied and sheltered, the men suffered starvation, frostbite, and all manner of disease. Most of their clothing was in tatters, but they mended and wore it all the same, for it was all they had.

The Prussian Baron Friedrich von Steuben had recently arrived and was posting sentries for the night, while Washington, in his small cabin, lit a candle and attended to the matter of how to provision his soldiers.

For Washington, the harsh conditions besetting his men dragged his own spirits down. Washington felt each blast of wind that tore at them, suffering for all rather than for only one. And he began to wonder if what they were doing could possibly succeed, whether a lost cause was worth so much suffering. Even the dispatch he was about to write to the Continental Congress had an air of futility about it: the representatives had vacated Philadelphia for York and had neither the money nor resources to provide relief.

Taking up his quill, the forty-four-year-old commander-in-chief began to write, hoping that someone who read his report might find a way to help.

As he wrote the date, Washington felt a chill, and turned to see if the fire in the hearth was burning out. To his amazement, there was a woman standing between him and the fire; despite her position, the flames were still visible. The woman was dressed in a white robe, her face tinged with a golden glow. The future president couldn't see her eyes, but he felt her gaze upon him.

He spoke to her, but the woman said nothing. Then, behind her, Washington suddenly saw a boat with Pilgrims, one of which, a young woman, he took to be her.

He rubbed his eyes in disbelief, but the image remained—and changed.

Next, he saw his own soldiers huddled around campfires, as clear to him as though the wall of his cabin had vanished. He saw colonial troops and French troops standing armed while British soldiers stacked their weapons in defeat. Next, he saw a plain, and canvas-topped wagons moving across it, then a black engine firing smoke toward the heavens as it raced along a metal road, and an ocean, gleaming as the sun set behind it. Iron navies and vast cities and great industry with people everywhere amongst them. And he saw a flag, not unlike the one his own troops carried, although there were far more stars on the canton. So *many* more.

Then, both the visions and the woman were gone.

The candle on his writing table had burned nearly all the way down. The quill was still in his hand, and the fire was subdued, yet he felt as if no time had passed. He put his fingers to his eyes and reflected on what had happened.

Washington knew that he'd seen the future of what he and his soldiers were fighting for, what the Continental Congress had called the United States of America. And he knew that he must never again think of giving up.

He returned to his dispatch and told no one of what he had seen. But, his spirit renewed, Washington found ways for his men to survive the winter. In the spring he formed an alliance with France which helped to hasten a colonial victory.

Washington rarely spoke of the ghost who had visited him that night at Valley Forge, but when he did, he said that she, as much as anyone, was responsible for the birth of the new nation.

# 1817: The Ghost of Robertson County

When John Bell first came to Robertson County, in northern central Tennessee, he survived by hunting. Only when he took a wife did he turn to the more stable livelihood of farming.

For nearly twenty years, John, his wife Emma, and later, their children, Betsy and John Jr., lived a life of peace and contentment. Then, late one night, they were awakened by a faint scraping at the kitchen door, as though a cat or opossum were trying to get in. John went downstairs to investigate, but when he arrived he found nothing—no animal, not even tracks in the soil.

The following night the same thing happened, though this time the scratching was more insistent. Once again, John went to see what was causing the ruckus, but there was nothing at the door.

Each night for the next two nights, the sounds grew

louder. Finally, on the fifth night, John decided to sit downstairs in the kitchen, a shotgun across his knees. This time, the instant the sounds began, he ran to the door and flung it open; once more, however, there was only the night. At least, that was all he could see.

On the sixth night, John and his son elected to wait outside, hoping to get off a shot at who or what came to the door. But at nearly half past midnight, the sound they heard was not the sound they'd been expecting.

Upstairs, at the other end of the house, thirteen-year-old Betsy began to shriek. Her mother and the men arrived at her bed, and while Emma lit candles around the room, John and John Jr. listened as something clawed at the bedroom wall—from the inside.

"Sweet Lord," John moaned. "Whatever it is, I must have let it in."

He went over and rapped on the wall, and the sounds stopped. Suddenly, Betsy shrieked again: there was something moving under her blankets, raking her legs. Her father leapt on the bed, swept the covers into his arms, and slammed them repeatedly against the floor. While he still held the bundle tightly, Emma began to wail and reach behind her, screaming that something was pinching her back.

John Jr. ran over and slapped at her housecoat, but there was nothing there. And as quickly as the attack had begun, it was over.

The next morning, the farmer called on the local pastor, James Matthew Johnson, to tell him what had happened. Admitting that the unwanted visitor could be of infernal origins, and agreeing to bless the room, Johnson went back with the farmer, and standing beside the girl's bed, he opened his prayer book and began reciting from Ephesians, about the children of wrath.

Johnson continued his vigil until sunset, at which time they had dinner. The preacher said he would remain with the Bells until after midnight to make certain his prayer had been effective.

Long after dinner, while John and the clergyman sat in the small, firelit living room reading from their respective

Bibles, they heard a heavy, scurrying sound on the floor above their heads. They ran upstairs, hearing Betsy's cries nearly drowning out the low snarling, which had begun at the same time.

When they arrived, the men saw Betsy's hands darting from her face to her legs and back. Something hulking and dark blurred the shadows beyond the bed, though they couldn't make out its features.

"Papa, it's *biting* me!"

His hands trembling, the preacher opened his Bible while John ran to his daughter and threw himself on top of her. Emma and John Jr. arrived moments later and blocked the doorway.

Holding the Bible before him but reciting from memory, the clergyman said in a broken voice, "Above all, taking the shield of faith, wherewith ye shall be able to quench all the fiery darts of the wicked—"

At once, the attack stopped and the blur vanished. Suddenly, the pages of the Bible were slashed, as if by razors, and the book flew from the preacher's hands. It was dragged across the floor and then flung against the wall, where it came apart.

Sobbing, Betsy hugged her father; no one else moved.

The next morning, the pastor implored John to move his family from the farm, into the church, until something could be done about the foul presence. John refused to leave his home, stating that if God had singled him out for this affliction, he would not run from it.

Emma understood, but asked, at least, that Betsy might be allowed to leave. John permitted her to go with the preacher, as much to protect her as to stop gossip he had heard in town when the haunting began, talk that suggested his daughter was a witch.

The following night, the family waited up together, not with shotguns or Bibles, but simply holding hands and hoping that whatever was plaguing them would find no sport in the empty chamber, and that it would leave as suddenly as it had come.

Shortly after midnight, they heard a heavy padding upstairs in their daughter's room. Their hearts raced, fingers tightening in one another's grip. The bed creaked and there was a long silence, followed once again by ponderous footfalls.

The sound moved toward the staircase.

John Jr. rose slowly. "I'm going to open the door. Maybe it'll leave."

"Maybe it will follow Betsy," Emma cautioned.

The young man stopped on the bearskin rug that lay just inside the door. John Sr.'s eyes drifted toward it, the hide of a bear he'd once shot for its fat.

A guttural roar turned their heads toward the bottom of the staircase. The darkness was blurred by a form moving just beyond the edge of the firelight. It was more massive than the night before, nearly twice the size.

The intruder suddenly darted into the light, its shadowy mass landing on John Jr. and knocking him to the floor. The boy's father grabbed his shotgun and fired above his son, into the hazy form, but the attacker was unhurt.

As Emma screamed, the farmer impulsively lowered his sights and shot the bearskin. There was an awful howl, and the attack abruptly ceased. The Bells stood still in the sudden silence.

"What happened?" Emma asked.

"It's come for what belongs to it."

"For what?"

"For its skin. I hunted it, and God help us, Emma, now it's hunting us."

The room was quiet, and setting the gun aside, the farmer went to the pelt, gathered it in his arms, and pushed it into the fireplace.

The following night, Emma and John retired as usual, both of them falling asleep quickly, the strain of the previous days having taken its toll.

Shortly after midnight, John was awakened by something brushing against his shinbones. Warily, he lifted the covers and looked down: he saw nothing, but there was a musky smell, and the pressure crawled up his legs to his chest.

"Oh God!" he gasped, and his wife awoke. She heard her husband raling and, lighting a candle, saw him clutching at his chest.

"John, what is it?"

The farmer was unable to speak. Emma made a paste for his chest, but the pressure didn't leave until dawn, at which time she sent for the doctor. The physician prepared a draught to relieve the pressure, and the following night, when John woke up choking, his wife gave it to him.

The farmer had difficulty swallowing, but when it finally went down, he relaxed—and began to feel dizzy.

"Emma—"

She stroked his hair.

"Emma, the ghost . . ."

She froze and looked at him with confusion. "No, John. It isn't here."

John began to grow cold. He shook his head weakly.

"Poison."

"John?" She shook him lightly as his eyes shut.

*"He* did it . . . and he will return every generation to punish me. . . ."

That was the last thing John Bell uttered. He died in his wife's arms.

When the doctor came, he pronounced the farmer dead and examined the phial. He told John Jr. that the syrupy liquid was not the medicine he'd prepared. Somehow, it had been changed into some kind of poison made from what looked like tree sap.

The hauntings stopped that night.

Eventually, John Jr. and Betsy married and had children of their own. More than a decade after their father's death, both heard scratching at the doors of their homes.

At their mother's insistence, each had retained an unburnt section of the bear's pelt, and when they heard the sounds, they slipped quietly from bed, went to the kitchen, and set the fur afire. As it burned, there was a small howl, and then the scratching stopped.

The ghost never reappeared, nor have any other hunters ever reported being stalked, in turn, by their prey. But then, none had ever hunted in a wood sacred to the Creek Indians and to their vengeful bear-god.

## 1834: The Unknown Patriot

During the War of 1812, eight thousand British troops marched down the Mississippi River toward New Orleans, where they were met by American militiamen hiding behind bales of cotton. In a half-hour, one-quarter of the British force was either dead, wounded, or captured, with the loss of only eight American lives.

One of the men should not have died.

His name is unknown. He was a twenty-year-old American officer who, in order to spy on the enemy, took a uniform from a dead English regular and tried to infiltrate the British ranks. Spotted by American lookouts, he was captured; when American battle plans were found in his pocket, he was charged with spying.

The young man was brought before Major Jean Le-Clerque who, with the battle over, was more interested in drinking than in hearing stories from spies. LeClerque refused to listen to the captive's explanation and had him put before a firing squad and executed. The soldier died swearing vengeance.

His body was turned over to the British, and when he couldn't be identified, he was buried in an unmarked grave in a field outside the city.

After the war, LeClerque left the military, settled in New Orleans, and opened a tavern. He married a local woman and had a son, Andre.

On the occasion of Andre's twentieth birthday, his father threw him a big party at the tavern, after which his son continued the celebration with friends at a local brothel. Andre had just gone upstairs with an attractive French girl when he heard someone calling his name in a slow, almost drawling voice.

He looked around, saw no one in the small, richly appointed room.

*"Qu'est-ce que c'est?"* his companion asked.

"It's nothing," he said, and returned to her arms.

"LeClerque."

The young man started, and once again looked around. This time he climbed from the small four-poster and pulled open the door, but there was no one in the corridor. He stalked to the open French windows and looked behind the drapes, then pulled open the doors of the broad tulipwood cabinet.

"LeClerque."

The voice was coming from outside. Leaning out the window, the youth looked down and saw no one.

"This isn't amusing!" he said.

"LeClerque."

The speaker was somewhere below and, running from the room, Andre dressed and hurried down the steps and out onto the cobbled street.

Now there was a man standing there, a young man wearing the costume of a British soldier. There were several holes in the jacket, all of them around the heart. The man had the sallow skin and vacant expression of one who had been ill.

The girl came to the window and called down, but Andre

ignored her. He regarded the man suspiciously. "Was it you who called me?"

The man nodded once.

"Have you no decency, man? I'm with a lady."

"You are needed," the man said, his voice as hollow and expressionless as his eyes.

"By whom? Did Father send you?"

The figure turned slowly and pointed down the road, toward the field beyond.

"What? Who needs me? *Who?*"

A moment later, Andre found himself standing alone, looking down the empty street. Thinking he'd had too much to drink, he was about to go back inside when he saw the man standing on a rise in the middle of the hill. The figure raised an arm and beckoned. Sighing with disgust, Andre motioned up to the girl to wait, and started down the street.

Muttering under his breath, he reached the point where the man had been only to find him gone again.

Standing there with his hands on his hips, Andre turned around several times, kicked at the soil, then shouted, "You'll pay for this, my drunk friends!" He started back toward the brothel, complaining about the prank.

He stopped when he saw the figure standing in front of him. The redcoat was just a few feet away, a musket cradled in his arms.

"There you are!" Andre sneered. "I thought you said someone needed me." A smile pulled at the ends of his mouth. "Or is this some sort of ruse for my birthday? Did Thomas and John put you up to this?"

The figure raised the gun slowly. Andre's smile collapsed.

"What are you doing?"

He aimed at the young man's heart.

"This is *not* funny!"

Andre stared down the barrel for a long moment before starting to back away.

"Wait. *Wait!*"

A gunshot stopped his retreat, blowing him to the ground and echoing down the silent streets.

Within a few minutes, men with lanterns were converging upon the spot where they'd heard the blast. Jean LeClerque was among them.

The men found Andre lying dead upon the field. There was no sign of violence, no bloodshed, only a look of sheer terror on his face—and one thing more. Andre was wearing the tattered uniform of a British infantryman, a uniform whose jacket had five holes over the heart.

The shock of seeing his son dead cost Jean LeClerque his own life.

The French girl, watching from the window, had seen everything, but no one believed her story. Nor did it matter. The unknown patriot had been avenged.

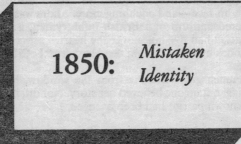

# 1850: *Mistaken Identity*

The small church overlooked the Long Island Sound, whose sparkling waters often brought the salty smell of the Atlantic to the peaceful town of Stratford, Connecticut.

Presbyterian Reverend Clinton Phelps enjoyed riding to the water's edge and then walking along the rocky shore, contemplating the subject of his next sermon or perhaps a personal problem a member of his congregation had presented to him.

One day, the preacher brought his oldest son Tad to the shore, so the clergyman could better understand what was important to young men the age of fifteen. They talked, ate the fruit his wife, Virginia, had packed for them, and watched the small waves washing ashore.

Toward the end of their talk, Tad suddenly looked around. He heard voices, though he saw no one nearby. When his father asked if anything were wrong, the young man dismissed the distraction with a laugh.

That night, during dinner, Tad heard the voices again. Once again, they were muffled, as though spoken from behind a mask, and he couldn't make out the words.

"Is something the matter, Tad?" his mother asked.

Before Tad could answer, his younger brother Thomas rose and pointed to the fireplace; everyone turned.

Behind the table, the poker, log fork, and fire shovel were standing straight up beside the coal hod. After a moment, they began moving slowly, up and down, tapping against the floor. Lying beside them, the bellows closed slowly, then inflated again.

Reverend Phelps went to investigate, but his wife laid a hand on his arm.

"It's all right," he said. "I'm sure there is an explanation."

As he approached, the fire suddenly ignited, chunks of coal flew at him from the hod, and his wife, sons, and baby daughter Elizabeth were pelted with potatoes from the table. A pair of silver candlesticks began thumping loudly up and down on a shelf in the kitchen, then jumped to the floor and continued pounding until they shattered.

Ducking the swift-flying coals, the reverend ran back, scooped up his daughter, and carried her upstairs, followed by the rest of the family. They ran into the master bedroom and shut the door—Virginia gasping when she saw clothing from her closets arranged into the shape of twelve women kneeling in prayer.

Suddenly, Tad heard voices more clearly.

*"Pray ye, lad, pray!"*

"Did you hear that?" he asked the others.

His father said nothing. He had gone to the clothing and, silently mouthing the Lord's Prayer, tentatively touched one figure on the shoulder. The clothes sagged, and he poked the blouse harder. This time the garment fell to the ground; he quickly deflated the other women in turn. While his wife and Thomas gathered the clothing, all of them trying not to pay attention to the racket downstairs, Reverend Phelps turned to Tad. "No, son. Did we hear what?"

"People telling me . . . to pray." Tad touched his forehead. "Father, I . . . I see them, now. Men on the beach— young men."

The reverend stared at his son, resisting the urge to take him by the hand and pull him to the church to pray, as the voices had bidden.

The boy shut his eyes. "They're pulling a boat to shore. I see one man taking two pistols from his girdle. He's aiming at the other two . . . and firing. Now they've fallen, and he's going to the boat alone.

"There are fabrics. Silk."

"Smugglers," the clergyman muttered. "These are the spirits of the damned."

"Now he's leaving with the goods . . . a young man . . . thin . . ."

The color left the reverend's face. "Like you, son? Like *you?*"

The young man was unable to answer. He was staring ahead, lost in his vision, and though his father shook him, he couldn't be awakened.

Leaving him, the reverend ran downstairs and stepped boldly into the kitchen. The fireplace tools and candlesticks were still drumming, and as soon as the preacher entered, the coals and potatoes came hurtling at him again.

"He is not the one you want!" Phelps screamed. "The man you seek is long dead!"

Tongues of flame shot from the fireplace and licked the iron implements.

"I tell you, he is *not* the one who betrayed you! This boy is *my son!* He is not one of you!"

Pots came tumbling from cabinets, and plates spun atop neat stacks, then crashed one after another against the walls. Flames shot along the floor like serpents' tongues.

And the preacher realized, suddenly, that it wasn't his son they wanted.

Racing upstairs, the reverend went to his wife's sewing room, gathered up the finest fabric she had there, and went downstairs, where the fireplace was now blazing with the intensity of a furnace. Reverend Phelps dropped the cloth in the center of the floor, then moved a broom and chairs back from the flames.

*"Here!"* he yelled, holding both hands toward the fabric. "Here is what you came for!"

The din continued, and sheets of flame blazed across the

cloth without burning it. A chunk of coal struck Reverend Phelps's forehead and, though dazed, he tried to understand what else he could possibly do to keep the wraiths from his son.

What would they want, short of vengeance? What could he give to the spirits of smugglers?

Turning, he ran to a cupboard and took out his purse, and that of his wife, both of which he dropped onto the fabric. Then he grabbed a silver goblet and laid it there as well. After a long moment, everything fell still and silent, save for the fire. Then, with a noise that sounded ominously like a laugh, the fire swept over the offering and set it ablaze.

The flames jumped high, nearly to the ceiling timbers. The clergyman called to Thomas and sent him outside to fill buckets with water. Reverend Phelps himself stayed close to the blaze, though he didn't stamp it out. He let it burn, only stamping sparks which landed outside the perimeter of the cloth and money.

When Thomas returned, the minister kept the buckets beside him, though he had a feeling he wouldn't need them. And sure enough, when the goods he had laid before the specters were consumed, the flame died on its own.

All was silent. There was only the faintest odor of salt in the air.

The reverend went upstairs feeling unclean for having bartered with the damned—the ghosts of smugglers, no less. But as he held his eldest son to him, these feelings left, and the holy man felt only gratitude.

The ghosts never returned, though neither the reverend nor any member of his family ever went walking on the beach again.

## 1855: More Than Banquo's Ghost

In the middle of the nineteenth century, an odd little mix of establishments could be found on the corner of Chestnut Street and Sixth in Philadelphia, a short walk from Independence Hall, the birthplace of the nation.

One next to the other, there were a shooting gallery, the Shakespeare Bowling Saloon, the Melodeon with its "celebrated troupe of dancers," and the Chestnut Street Theatre, its four-columned facade and elegant interior hosting a variety of alternately distinguished and popular plays.

In 1855, the playhouse was presenting *Faint Heart,* a comedy of manners largely forgotten, save for what happened during an evening performance.

The female star, Julia Daly, was alone on stage, performing before a full house, when props in the parlor-set began moving of their own accord. At first, the drapes on the wall began to blow. Then an empty teacup was overturned in the actress's hand, and a chair tipped over. Finally, the curtain came loose and rolled shut with a thud.

While the audience sat there in confused silence, a sonorous voice seemed to rush along every row.

*"Dear Jesus!"* it said. *"The theater! Save it!"*

The slender, nervous theater manager immediately came out and made apologies for "difficulties backstage." The performance resumed a half-hour later, and there were no further disruptions.

After a thorough search of the theater turned up no hidden wires or lurking pranksters, the manager and one of the theater's owners, young William Burton, decided that someone must have made a bet at the saloon that he could disrupt the play and get away with it.

However, old Dublin-born stagehand Caleb Paight was not so sure. He stopped Burton as the man was headed for his carriage.

"Sir," said the elderly man, "I'm not sure what you're going to think of me, but I believe I know that voice."

"A drinking partner, no doubt?"

"No, sir, though I'm not sure I trust what I heard."

Burton said impatiently, "And what do you think you heard?"

"A dead man, sir."

"How nice." Sneering, Burton turned toward his carriage.

Caleb walked after him. "I was working on the night in '22 when the first Chestnut burned down. James Rhodes was playing Macbeth. He died trying to save the theater when the fire broke out. It was at 9:45, sir, the same hour as what happened tonight."

Burton entered his carriage, dismissing what the stagehand had told him.

The following day, a thorough search of the theater was made once again, and prior to the performance guards were stationed at each door.

Before the show, the somber manager gathered his personnel around and announced that, the previous day, the property had been sold; this was to be the final presentation, and the final performance, at the Chestnut Street Theatre, which was going to be razed.

Though the cast was disappointed and the stagehands devastated, the show went on as planned.

As Miss Daly reached her soliloquy, she made a point of sitting on the chair which had fallen over. The few people who had been in the audience the night before quietly applauded. She smiled as she spoke.

Then the curtain rolled down.

And the voice once again drifted along the aisles.

*"Someone help! Where is your courage?"*

There were thumps and shouts from the wings, and while the audience murmured, Miss Daly came forward and did her soliloquy by the footlights. She had no choice: every piece of furniture had been upended.

When the set was repaired, the theater's final performance continued without incident.

The following day, the stagehands were brought in to begin removing props, equipment, and fixtures from the theater. The work continued well past dark. When the crew was told to go home for the night, Caleb remained behind.

With all the lights shut down, he sat in the middle of the orchestra and waited.

He passed the time by reminiscing, thinking back to the awful fire and how the actor perished. It was funny how the stagehands had mourned him. He wasn't just one of the great American actors of his day—the first to gain the grudging admiration of English critics for his interpretations of Shakespeare—he was also a man who appreciated the work of the crews, uncharacteristic recognition from a usually self-impressed breed.

Soon, the deep voice once again wafted through the theater.

*"To me . . . bring water. . . ."*

In the pitch darkness, Caleb saw a white shadow materialize at center stage and move slowly to the wings. Bolting from his seat, the old stagehand followed it.

*"Save her . . . save the theater!"*

The shapeless cloud moved slowly behind the proscenium, toward the back of the theater, where a fallen lantern had started the blaze thirty-three years before.

Caleb walked to where the glow was moving along the brick wall.

"It can't be done, Mr. Rhodes. You can't save her this time, either."

The cloud stopped.

"I'll miss her too, sir. But they're going to put something else here. It's progress."

A wall of cold descended swiftly, raising goosebumps on Caleb's arms and neck; a noise, low and forlorn, echoed through the blackness. As it died, the cloud, too, faded. Soon both were gone.

Caleb told his story only to a few friends and family members, though no one ever believed him. But that didn't really bother him. When the theater was razed, he snuck off with a small piece of stageboard which had survived the original fire, and kept it until his death.

Progress could not take that memento from him.

Nor, he was sure, from James Rhodes.

# 1862: *Still Hiding*

Kinderhook is a town located some twenty miles southeast of Albany, New York. One of the area's most historic buildings is Lindenwald House, a small but stately former residence of retired president Martin Van Buren.

In 1861, twenty-one years after losing the White House because of his unpopular economic views, the seventy-nine-year-old Van Buren was working on his memoirs in the study of the old mansion. Walls of light came through the windows, and the sweet music of birds drifted from the trees outside the room.

Writing at a small table, the former president was startled to see a man sitting across from him. In the bright light, it was difficult to make out his features, but he was elderly and well-dressed, in a style like that of some two decades before.

Van Buren said quietly, "Who are you, sir, and who admitted you?"

"Billy," said the old man. "Billy brought me here."

Van Buren thought for a moment. "I know no Billy," he said, and rose to get his son John, who was visiting from New York.

As he rose, the well-dressed man rose with him. The stranger left ahead of the elderly president, through the open door.

More startled than anything, Van Buren followed him. The figure was walking toward the staircase which led upstairs.

"Who are you?" he asked again.

"Everyone knows who I am," the figure replied without turning, "and who I might have been," he added mournfully.

Van Buren did not follow, but called his son, who came from upstairs. He said no one had come up there, and though he searched every room, he could not find the man his father had seen. John suggested that his father sit in the garden for a while.

Relaxing on a lawn chair in the back of the house, Van Buren dozed off. Some time later, he was awakened by a sigh, and opened his eyes to see the man sitting beside him. He could see the man's face now, which was gaunt, scowling, bespectacled—and familiar. He was gazing longingly across the yard.

Van Buren sat up. "You are persistent."

"That has been noted before."

"It doesn't surprise me. Will you tell me, now, who you are?"

The figure looked at him. "You do not know?"

"I do not, though I confess, I seem to know you from somewhere. Did we meet when I was a senator, perhaps?"

"Then, and at other times."

"Were we allies?"

"I had no friends, sir. None, save for Billy."

"Who is this Billy?" Van Buren demanded.

John came out then, and when Van Buren turned to point out the stranger, the old man was gone.

Disturbed by the encounters, Van Buren retired early that night, only to be awakened by a presence in the room. When he looked into the dark chamber, he dimly perceived the figure, hands clasped behind his back, standing by the window and staring out into the night.

"They did not understand why I challenged him," the man said without being asked, and without turning. "The insults he expected I should bear! And then later, who did call upon me when I lost my beloved wife, or my poor young grandson, or my dear, dear daughter Theodosia. I was alone, and all else I had done was forgotten."

The former president thought for a moment, and then his eyes grew wide.

"Dear Lord, it's not possible."

"What, sir, is not?"

"It cannot be—*you* cannot be."

"Who, sir?"

"Mr. Burr!"

The figure turned now. "If I did not resemble him, still would you know me by my suffering. There was so much left undone. So very much."

Before Van Buren could think of what more to say, or even if he should say anything at all to such an apparition, John entered.

"Were you calling, Father?"

"Only in my sleep," the old man said.

His son smiled and left, but now the figure was gone, never to return in the few months left in Van Buren's life.

His son, to whom he eventually told the tale, remarked that it was nothing more than his father's tired mind reacting to the chore of editing his memoirs, of living so much in the past.

Yet, the fact is that in 1804, at the time of Burr's duel with the much-liked Alexander Hamilton, Lindenwald was owned by the Van Ness family. Young Billy Van Ness was the vice-president's second. After the shooting, it was believed that Burr and Billy rode to Lindenwald, and that the vice-president remained in hiding there for several weeks, though this could never be proven, until shortly after the turn of the century. Exploring every corner of the home, its new owner, Dr. B. H. Birney, entered a long-unused attic. Opening the room, he went inside and found it empty.

Empty, that is, save for a calling card belonging to the man who had been closeted there, Aaron Burr.

(Note: Van Buren's ghost has often been seen wandering through the mansion's garden, while the restless spirit of the monumentally ambitious Burr has also been seen at the Octagon House in Washington, D.C., and in the Jumel Mansion in New York City. Finally, it is of some historical interest to note that while visiting Lindenwald, author Washington Irving first heard a popular local tale, the saga of a headless horseman.)

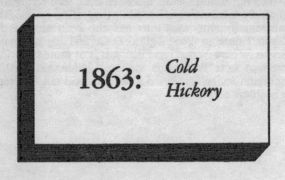

# 1863: *Cold Hickory*

*I felt a hand on the back of my chair. It was the ghost of Andrew Jackson.*

—*Mary Todd Lincoln*

Usually, Mrs. Lincoln was the one who was away.

Preoccupied with the business of war, President Abraham Lincoln rarely departed from his routine. She, on the other hand, would spend days shopping in New York, visiting friends in the country, or even closeting herself for days in another bedroom because she had had a quarrel with the president.

This time, it was Mr. Lincoln who was gone, having left on November the 18th to deliver an address at the consecration of the soldiers' cemetery at Gettysburg.

Now Mrs. Lincoln was sitting in a chair beside a card table, a young woman to her left, and her devoted mulatto seamstress Elizabeth Keckley to her right. The drapes had been taken down at Mrs. Lincoln's insistence, and it was nearly nine P.M., the room dark. Though Elizabeth said nothing to the First Lady, her expression made it clear that she wanted no part of what was about to transpire.

The First Lady could also imagine what Abraham would think of all this. He'd call it mad or devilish, or worse, but she didn't care.

A year before, in 1862, their twelve-year-old son Willie had caught a cold and died. Since then, not a day had passed that she didn't cry—of late, in private, for her husband had warned that if she cried too much, she would go mad. And, going mad, she would be placed in an asylum.

Yet, she could not stop. And she refused to take off her black mourning gown and veil. For despite what the Reverend Francis Vinton had insisted, despite what her own husband proclaimed, she had to *know*, for a fact, that Willie was in heaven, in the arms of God. She would go mad if she did not.

The third woman at the table was a medium, Clara Frayser, who had been recommended to Mrs. Lincoln by her nephew, Lockwood Todd. Mrs. Lincoln had waited for her husband to leave before summoning the woman from Philadelphia to the White House.

A pale, severe-looking woman, Clara lit a scented candle in the middle of the table, then told the other women that they must all join hands, and not speak unless permission was expressly granted.

Mrs. Lincoln agreed, then watched as Clara shut her eyes and sat stiffly in the wooden chair. After a moment, the woman slumped and her breathing slowed.

Mrs. Lincoln hoped that their preparations had been sufficient. Everything soft, not just the drapes but the mattress and cushioned armchairs, had been removed from the bedroom—anything that might absorb the spiritual presence or make it difficult for ethereal visitors to make their presence felt. She had been told that if they were lucky, and the spirits were active, they would hear raps on the table in answer to simple yes-or-no questions, though it wasn't impossible that a spirit would actually communicate through Clara. The First Lady resisted the urge to pray, knowing well that in God's sight what she was doing was wrong.

She had no idea how much time had passed. Oblivious to the seamstress, Mrs. Lincoln watched the medium intently. Finally, Clara sat up stiffly, and in a voice lower and more sonorous than her own, she said, "There is a shade among us."

Mrs. Lincoln squeezed Elizabeth's hand tightly. The seamstress pressed her knees together to keep them from shaking.

"It is a man," Clara went on, "an elderly man, and he wishes to help. Ask your questions."

Mrs. Lincoln thanked God anyway. She swallowed, and tried to compose herself; Clara had warned her to remain calm, lest she frighten any spirits.

"How, how is my Willie?" she asked.

A strong male voice came from the medium's lips. "He shares in the glory of the Lord."

The First Lady laughed and sobbed at once, and it was several seconds before she could speak again. "Is he here, with us?"

"No."

"Can you *bring* him? Can I hear his voice!"

"No."

Used to being pampered, Mrs. Lincoln demanded, "Why *not?*"

Elizabeth tightened her grip on Mrs. Lincoln's hand, a tacit reminder of what Clara had said about retaining her composure.

Mrs. Lincoln nodded, then asked, "Who are you?"

"Your son's guardian."

"Do you have a name?"

"Yes."

"Can you tell it to me?"

Mrs. Lincoln suddenly felt a chill on her neck, as though a block of ice had touched it. She didn't turn until Elizabeth let out a cry, one which would have been considerably louder had the seamstress's lips not been pressed together.

The First Lady craned her head around, and unlike Elizabeth, was filled with joy rather than fear.

Behind her, looking exactly as he did in his portrait at the

White House, and in the daguerreotype she had seen, was the figure of President Andrew Jackson.

The white-haired man looked benignly at her, and she smiled back, content. Who better to look after her boy than Old Hickory, a man who was like her husband in so many ways?

She turned and looked again at Clara. "Can you . . . will you tell my Willie that his parents love him, and that we will love him always?"

The spirit's voice answered, "Yes."

There was a long silence, after which Clara slumped again, and slowly came from her trance. Mrs. Lincoln had trouble opening her hands, her fingers stiff from clenching them so tightly. She apologized to Elizabeth, who was rubbing her own fingers to regain the circulation.

Exhausted by the experience, and having no recollection of the visitation, Clara asked what had happened. The First Lady told her she had spoken to her son's guardian, and that she was grateful for the serenity it had brought her. Clara offered to stay and, perhaps the next day, to try to communicate with Willie himself.

Mrs. Lincoln declined. "It's enough to know he's well," she said.

The following day, Mrs. Lincoln put away her mourning dress. She was at peace for the seventeen months which followed, at which point, sadly, she was to need the dress once again.

(Note: Mrs. Lincoln held many seances subsequent to this one and was also visited by the ghost of her brother Alexander, who died fighting for the Confederacy. Years later, a seamstress named Parks was working on a spread on the Andrew Jackson bed when a ghost came up behind her. She ran from the room without waiting to see whether it was President Jackson. Parks reports that the bed was the site of many hauntings.)

1864: *Buried Alive*

Dungeon Rock, in the Lynn Woods Reservation in Lynn, Massachusetts, has been haunted for over three hundred years.

In 1651, settlers along the Saugus River lived in fear of the pirate Thomas Veal and his men. For seven years, the pirates would boat up the river, demand food or clothing from the colonists, and then hide in a cave in the woods. In 1658, an earthquake caused the entrance to the cave to collapse, burying Veal alive. None of the citizenry mourned him, and stories began to circulate about a treasure Veal was believed to have buried near the cave. Reports of strange noises coming from the cave kept people from searching for it, though that didn't stop them from talking.

In 1851, undaunted by tales of noises and a possible ghost, one Hiram Marble undertook to find the gold, digging one hundred and fifty feet into the ground in search of it. If there was a ghost, it didn't disturb him; if it disturbed him, he was greedy enough to ignore it. However, after thirteen years, and having spent every cent he had on the project, he was forced to discontinue his quest. He even speculated to one friend that the ghost kept moving the treasure.

Though Marble's dramatic failure dissuaded others from taking over where he had left off, the cave still held an eerie fascination, especially for the young. In 1864, a year after Marble gave up his quest, a pair of twelve-year-old boys decided to camp out beside the pit to see if the ghost would appear.

Zachary was the braver of the two, a gangly boy who walked with a six-foot-long stick, like a prophet, but which he could also use to defend himself. Mostly, though, he used it to harass his chubby companion, Benjamin, hitting him on the rear. Benjamin had a remarkable sense of direction, finding water or a bee's hive for honey—or the way home— very easily.

Benjamin was also good at finding his way in the dark, which was one of the reasons Zachary bravely suggested their little venture. If the ghost showed up, they could always break camp and run home.

The sun didn't go down until after nine, by which time the campfire they'd lit at dinnertime was nearly extinguished. The pit and the sealed mouth of the cave were less than fifty yards from where they lay on their backs, looking up at the stars.

Saying their prayers—lest they fall asleep and invite disaster—they talked of what they'd heard about the pirate, which was a great deal, and what they knew about the pirate, which was considerably less.

What they'd *heard* was that Veal hadn't died screaming or repentant, but that he'd laughed as the rocks enclosed him, laughed that it had finally taken God himself to capture him. And that it was as much his laughter as his blasphemy which had cursed him to roam the earth for eternity.

Zachary was the first to suggest that they talk about something else, like making pictures out of the stars visible beyond the swaying treetops. An owl interrupted his own description of a smiling face, and he suggested they go to sleep instead.

Benjamin suggested they go down into the pit.

Zachary was glad he wasn't facing his friend, because he knew what his expression showed. It showed the fear that almost brought the corn pone they'd had for dinner back up his throat.

But he didn't want his friend to know he was afraid, and said that climbing down would be an adventure, hoping he could convince himself of that fact.

The first thing they did was drop a rock down. When it hit, Benjamin announced that it hadn't flooded since old man Marble left it, and would be safe. They chose straws to see who would go down first. Zachary won. Which meant he lost. He was first man down the steps.

The pit was over six feet across, and the wooden steps zigzagged down the center. Zachary walked in the dark, planting both feet on a step before continuing, nearly losing his balance several times as Benjamin bumped into him. He complained, but not too loudly: their voices echoed down here, and that sent chills along his back. Benjamin enjoyed the echo, and hooted several times to hear it come back at him. Each time, Zachary told him to be quiet, saying he was listening to make sure the steps were sturdy.

Eventually, they reached the bottom, and Zachary felt better. Until he realized that there was a sound coming from the other side of the wall.

Benjamin pointed out that that was where the cave was, and squeezed around Zachary to put his ear to the wall.

He reported that there was a clinking sound, like water falling a long way and hitting a puddle or a rock—

Or coins dropping into a pile.

Zachary said that if they were coins, Marble would have chopped through and investigated. Benjamin pointed out that maybe he never heard them. That maybe he never was down here at night.

Zachary wished he weren't either, and made no secret of the fact. He suggested they go, because if it were water, there could be a flood at any moment.

Benjamin told him he wanted to listen a little longer, that if there were treasure here, he wanted to come back for it. And would Zachary please put down his damned stick?

Zachary said he didn't have his stick.

Benjamin said, then, would he stop hitting him in the rear?

Zachary said his hands were in the pockets of his coveralls.

Benjamin bolted for the steps.

The boys ran up, stumbling, then shouting with fright when they heard what sounded like laughter. It may have been the echo of their own footsteps, or of their cries or panting, but it seemed to be louder than the sounds they made.

Though they hadn't gone far, they were desperately short of breath, and their legs ached, but they dared not rest. Then something brushed Zachary's right arm and he ran up, pushing past Benjamin; the heavyset boy lost his footing and fell back, dropping down into the pit.

Zachary heard him cry, but didn't stop. He ran to the opening of the pit, continued through the woods to the nearest house. He returned with three men, a lantern, and rope.

The men called down to Benjamin, and there was a weak response. They went down, following the lantern, Zachary trailing behind them. When they reached the bottom, they found Benjamin barely conscious, his legs and an arm badly broken. They also found rats, coming and going from the cave through a small opening at the base of the pit.

Binding Benjamin's broken limbs using the rope and slats from the steps, the men slowly carried him back to the mine entrance.

Months later, when Zachary and Benjamin spoke of the incident, Zachary told his friend what he had also seen in the light of the lantern.

There were fresh footprints in the corner of the pit; they belonged to none of the men. One of the prints was nothing more than the impression of a heel, the rest of it disappearing into the wall. And the rats, he said, were too small, by far, to have touched Benjamin. Nothing would ever convince the boys that it wasn't Veal's ghost which had accosted them.

Bars were later placed over Marble's pit, and to this day, no one who has gone poking around the area has found Veal's treasure. Many, though, claim to have found Veal, heard his demonic laughter, and felt the touch of his cutlass.

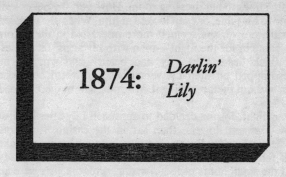

# 1874: *Darlin' Lily*

Joshua Johnson was a bank teller on the Barbary Coast in San Francisco, a small, goateed, very prim man who lived by himself in a room behind the bank.

A widower, the forty-one-year-old had come from Pittsburgh a year before, determined to start a new life following the death of his wife. She, Anna, the daughter of the bank president, had been a naggingly parsimonious woman, to whom a good time was salvaging what wood she could from the fireplace in order to use it again.

She died of pneumonia, refusing to take even as much of the curative tonic as the physician had prescribed for her.

Joshua had found the job through an acquaintance in San Francisco, who told him of this position. The teller liked the freewheeling lifestyle here; he especially liked Lily Vernon, a young dancer who worked at the Pot of Gold Casino. He talked about her at work and dreamt of her at night.

More than once, he had tried to get her attention by

sending lilies to her dressing room. However, she never sent a note to his table, or even looked at him. When she mingled with the crowd, she seemed more interested in the sailors who came in for the night—men with big arms, fat purses, and thick heads. Yet Lily had beauty *and* wit, for he eavesdropped on their conversations and heard her tease them without their realizing it. What she saw in them eluded him.

One night, Joshua decided to approach Lily after her last show. He sent flowers, then sat in the casino, fortifying himself with drink. But the fortification took longer to make itself felt than he'd expected, and he wasn't really ready until the small hours of the morning, after the girls were all gone and the casino was nearly empty.

"Now I smell like the rest of the men," he sniggered as he made his way around back, through a dirt alley. Opening the stage door, he stumbled down the corridor, then paused to listen. Swaying from too much drink, he heard her laughter coming from one of the rooms. He went over and knocked hard.

"Miss Vernon! Hellooo, Miss Vernon!"

She stopped laughing. The floorboards creaked and the door opened swiftly. Lily stood there, frowning.

"Good evening," Joshua said. Behind her, Joshua saw the flowers he'd sent. "Ah, I see you received my token. I was wondering—"

The woman slammed the door in his face.

Shaking his head with surprise and disbelief, the inebriated teller rapped again.

This time, at Lily's prompting, a man answered. He was big, bare-chested, and unhappy. He pushed Joshua against the wall, snarled, then shut the door again.

Fearful for Lily's safety alone with such a brute, Joshua regained his balance and, without knocking, opened the door and strode in.

The man and Lily were pressed together, her back to the wall, his face in her neck. Her hands were in his hair.

Certain Lily was being taken against her will, Joshua ran over to them, pounding the man's back with his fists. With a snarl, the bare-chested man turned, pushed Joshua back, grabbed the wooden chair by Lily's dressing table, and struck him hard across the chest.

The teller died as fragments of his rib cage perforated his heart. Tossing the chair aside, the big man threw Joshua over his shoulder, carried him outside, and dumped him in an outhouse which no one ever bothered using.

The next evening, before her first show, Lily was in her dressing room, repairing a tear in her pink dress for the Belle of the Mississippi number. She hadn't thought much of the events of the night before; men were always trying to see her, and were being "discouraged" by whomever she had chosen to be with. It wasn't her fault if, once in a while, things got out of hand. Neither weak men nor timid women had any business being here, as far as she was concerned.

As she sat there, Lily was surprised as the faint scent of lilies filled the room. She looked behind her to see if a flower hadn't fallen somewhere when the silly bouquet was removed the night before.

There was nothing, yet the odor remained, sweet and unmistakable.

Finishing up with the dress, she put it on and went to the door, as the smell was fast becoming stifling.

When she pulled the door open, she started: her annoying little suitor was standing there, a bouquet in his hand. She had *thought* that being knocked unconscious the night before would have dissuaded him, but apparently not.

Frowning, Lily noticed that the man didn't look quite the way he did when the sailor had carried him out. He was bone-white, his eyes and expression flat. And the flowers were overpowering. Calling for the stage boy, Lily shut the door and went to her dressing table.

She felt faint, and called for the stage boy again. The lilies were more pungent than any she had ever smelled. She loosened the tight collar of the dress and took a deep breath.

"I brought these for you," said a small voice, barely above a whisper.

Lily looked toward the door. It was shut, but the man was inside. He was walking toward her, the flowers extended. She rose and backed toward the far wall. She called once again for help. There was a knock at the door, the stage boy asking if he could come in.

"Yes!" she cried. "Come in."

The knob rattled. "It's locked, Miss Vernon."

"It *isn't!*"

"Should I break it down? Miss Vernon?"

The pale man came forward, and the room seemed to tilt. Or had it? As her lungs filled with the too-sweet air, her head grew light.

The stage boy was pounding on the door and calling her name. She heard, but couldn't answer. Her back was against the wall and she slid down, everything swirling and slowly turning to blackness. She saw the man's alabaster skin appear in the midst of the maelstrom, and then, unable to breathe, she saw nothing.

When the men broke down the door, Lily was unconscious. A doctor was summoned, and he was able to revive her using smelling salts. She told them about the man who had been there, and though a search was mounted, he was never found. Nor did anyone smell the lilies she swore had nearly choked her.

Joshua's ashen body was discovered two days later.

However, what surprised authorities was not that someone had been killed; that happened with some regularity on the Barbary Coast. What perplexed them was what they found in his hand.

Only Lily Vernon wasn't surprised to hear that he was clutching a bouquet of dead lilies.

# 1875: *Ghostly Passenger*

At first, the high school teacher thought it was one of her students.

Beatrice Mann had just moved to Vicksburg, Mississippi, and was one of the four chaperones who had accompanied students on a late-spring picnic to the Mississippi River. It was a misty morning, and sound travelled far and clearly on the damp air. So it was difficult, at first, for the young teacher to place the sound.

But when she heard it again, Beatrice turned to another young woman, the mother of one of the students, who was sitting on a blanket beside her.

"Is that one of the children?" Beatrice asked.

"Pardon me?" the other woman said, looking up from her needlepoint.

"I heard someone cry out. It sounded as though it came from the river."

Walking to the bank, Beatrice peered through the fleecy mist. The other woman followed.

"Do you see anything?" Beatrice asked.

The woman shook her head, then looked down the riverbank. "None of the children are near the river. Perhaps you heard an echo."

"It must have been," Beatrice said.

A few minutes later, two of her boys came over. "Miss Mann," said one, "we thought we heard something. It sounded like a woman calling for help."

"Show me," she said, and followed the students to a place where several old trees stood out over the water, like the fishing poles of some lazy giant.

"We were in the trees," said the youth, "and we heard someone calling on the opposite shore. We couldn't see anyone because of the mist, and we couldn't understand what she was saying."

"It was another language," said the other. "We could hear it clearly, but—"

The cry came again.

*"Aidez-moi! Mon Dieu, mon Dieu, les hommes me blessent!"*

"It's French," said the teacher. "I'm sure of it."

"What's she saying?" asked one of the boys.

"I don't know," Beatrice replied, "but I'm going to go for help."

Walking quickly down the riverbank, Beatrice rounded a bend and found an elderly man fishing in a rowboat. She explained what had happened, and asked if he would take her across. Nodding amiably and poking his pole in the bank, he ferried her over, then waited in his boat while she went into the woods. There was a strange smile on his lips.

Birds sang in the trees, and insects buzzed around Beatrice's face. She pressed into the woods, stepping quietly and listening.

Then she heard it again. The voice was coming from a small clearing ahead, and, picking up a heavy branch, Beatrice hurried over.

She found no one.

After looking around for a few minutes more, she reluctantly returned to the boat.

"Take me back quickly," she said. "I think someone's in danger."

They started back, the fisherman in no hurry. "You're new to Vicksburg, are you?" he asked.

Beatrice said she was, and asked if he couldn't row a little faster.

"Why? There's no one in danger, ma'am," he said.

"What are you saying? I heard—"

"I've heard the lady's voice too, many a time. Usually at this time o' day. But it's nothin' to be concerned with. Not any more."

Beatrice looked at him with surprise. "If she's in no danger, why does she—"

"Cry out? Oh, she *was* in danger, once." The fisherman rowed in long, easy strokes. "Y'see, a year ago—an' ya can ask any o' your youngsters, or look it up in the news-papers—a year ago, June, the riverboat *Iron Mountain* passed through here with over fifty passengers and a row o' barges tied to her stern. She passed through, but only the barges was ever found, floatin' downriver by Grand Gulf. The towlines'd been cut—not broken, just sliced away."

"What happened?"

"Some folks thought the great lady sunk, an' they searched for it. They searched because there was a lot of wealthy folk onboard, and a lot of jewels and gamblin' money that people would've liked to pocket. No wreckage was ever found, though people still say she sunk."

The fisherman reached the shore, but remained seated. Beatrice didn't move.

"I'll tell ya, ma'am, they didn't find it because there *wasn't* no wreckage. It was the work of river pirates. Musta been three dozen of 'em."

"How do you know?"

"Because I *saw* 'em! I was sleepin' on the far shore an' didn't move, lest they hear me. But I heard them. They stopped the boat and ordered everyone off, and then took what they wanted—includin' the women. Creole women."

Beatrice felt her skin crawl. The Creoles spoke French.

"They was screamin', but I couldn't understand what they was sayin'. An' they screamed all night, until just one was left—the woman you heard."

"She's still there?" Beatrice asked, confused.

The fisherman took back his pole while Beatrice got out.

"In a manner of speakin', ma'am. See, it's her ghost you heard. I seen 'em kill the passengers, then weight their bodies down with iron parts of the ship, and throw 'em in the river."

Now Beatrice was frowning. "Her ghost."

"Yes'm. You don't believe in 'em?"

"I don't. And what of the paddleboat?" she asked dubiously.

"The pirates took it apart," he said, pushing back into the river. "They carried away the pieces, then burned or buried 'em as they travelled."

The curious smile returned, and Beatrice no longer believed the old man's story. Angry for having wasted precious minutes, she returned to the picnic grounds, took her buggy into town, and stopped to see the sheriff.

Like the old man, he seemed unconcerned when she told her story.

"People've been reporting the cries for a year," he said, "an' each time we go out there, we don't see a thing."

"But there *was* a wreck, I understand. Perhaps someone is still in the woods. An old fisherman told me that pirates—"

"What old fisherman?" the sheriff asked.

"I don't know. He was old and short and—"

"Was he smiling? Wearin' a torn brown coat?"

Beatrice nodded.

The sheriff's brows arched. "If you saw him, ma'am, you should get yourself to church. Bass Cutler was the only man we *did* find when we went searchin' for the *Iron Mountain*. He was lyin' facedown on the far shore—his throat cut out. We never did find out who did it, any more than we could figger out what sunk the *Iron Mountain* or where she washed to."

Beatrice's mouth was dry as she asked, "Could it have been pirates?"

The sheriff was wearing a patronizing smile. "Now, it just could've been, but then, someone would've seen the boat downriver. A boat like that don't just disappear."

"What about the woman's voice? She just . . . 'is-appeared."

"She wasn't ever there," he said. "It's just a trick o' the wind and trees, that's all."

Beatrice didn't tell the sheriff what the old man had told her about the ship's fate. Somehow, she knew she must have dreamt it all. But she never went down to the river again. She preferred to believe that the horror the fisherman spoke of had never happened anywhere but in her imagination.

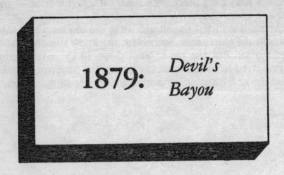

# 1879: Devil's Bayou

His name was Samuel Terry, and he was born shortly after his parents were freed from years of slavery.

Though cotton was all the elder Terrys knew, they refused to work it, not wanting to be reminded of the decade of backbreaking labor on the South Carolina plantation. Making their way southwest, to Louisiana, they built a small shack by the Calcasieu River, outside of Le Blanc, where Sam's father Joseph raised chickens, had a healthy garden, and also caught fish to feed his family.

Samuel was very good with animals, whether it was nursing sickly chickens or catching fish when his father couldn't. However, Samuel's heart was in frogs, and whenever he wasn't needed at home, he went into the marshes to see how many he could catch and add to his collection, which he kept in a fenced mud pit well behind the shack.

Not far from where the Terrys lived was a bayou. It had no

name, as far as they knew, but May Terry called it "the Devil's Bayou," because on still nights they could hear howling and shrieks which Joseph said were animals and May insisted were demons.

Samuel wanted to know which, and, one evening, telling his parents that he was going out to look for frogs, he continued past the marsh, toward the Devil's Bayou.

The sun had already set by the time the fourteen-year-old reached the edge of the bayou. Here, he proceeded cautiously, using a long branch to test the ground before he took each step. Finally, wading over to a small stretch of land in the middle of the still waters, he crouched and chewed on the mint leaves growing there.

There was no moon, and the stars were hidden by low clouds. Occasionally he heard noises which he knew were animal sounds: frogs belching, owls shrieking, and the distinctive clicking of giant water bugs. The air was thick and damp, but he didn't mind. He enjoyed being out here with animals, and he told himself that one day he would catch an owl to study it, see how it turned its head every which way.

Samuel's reverie was disturbed by a sloshing in the waters behind him. He turned and saw nothing, though now there were voices. It sounded to Samuel like people in a church, saying a prayer of some kind.

Deciding to get out of sight, he snuck back into the water until only the top of his head was above it. He sat still, on all fours, and watched intently as an orange glow grew between the trees.

After several minutes, a small group of people arrived carrying torches. He didn't recognize any of them, but they were obviously former slaves. He had heard, from a man whom they had given dinner to once, that many slaves had been brought here from a place called the West Indies. The man said he was from there, and he had the same kind of accent as these people.

The people—there were four of them—were walking right toward him. Slowly, silently, Samuel edged around the small island, hiding himself on the other side. He congratulated himself for his good sense: the people stopped just a few paces from where he'd been. There, they planted their torches in the island and took pouches from their belts, along with handfuls of small stick figures. The dolls were dressed strangely, some in costumes he'd never seen. He thought it odd that grown people should have dolls, and was curious to see what they did with them.

Suddenly, one of the four, an old woman, spoke.

"Tonight, it is our task to see that they suffer."

The others repeated what she'd said.

"Tonight, it is our task to see that they repent."

Once again, the others said the same thing.

"Tonight, it is our task to see that eternal rest is denied them."

The others said that too, and then all the people laid their figures on the water. They took a pinch of reddish powder from the pouches, sprinkled it on the figures, then stood back on the small muddy island.

Samuel was startled by what happened next. The water bubbled and sprayed upwards, and then bodies shot from the water—fully dressed bodies, writhing with pain, and shrieking like no people he'd ever heard. Some wore armor, like he'd once seen on a toy a white boy had; some were like the well-dressed plantation owners his parents often spoke of; some had clothing he didn't recognize at all, and carried whips or guns or clubs and other weapons. The fire from the torches seemed to lean toward them, then lash out at them, like long, monstrous fingers.

Any one of the men was enough to give Samuel bad dreams for a month. The men with beards and armor clenched their fists, turned their faces to the sky, and howled like wolves as their skin bubbled and burned. The three plantation owners whooped like cranes and tore at their faces until there was hardly any flesh left. And the men with weapons struck at one another, causing wounds and drawing blood and screaming with pain, but never falling. Watching them, Samuel shook so violently that waves filled the water around him, though no one seemed to notice amidst all the other turmoil.

The old woman spoke again. "Each night, those who have punished good people must themselves be punished."

The others repeated.

"Each night, the good dead must not be forgotten and the evil dead must not be allowed to forget."

The others chanted after her.

"Each night, those who have killed must not be allowed to die."

The others spoke, but by then the splashing water had washed away most of the powder on the dolls, and the wailing figures began to fade. As it mixed with the water, the powder looked to Samuel like blood. In a few moments, the awful creatures were gone, though the blood spread across the bayou.

Picking up their torches, the people said a prayer and then turned to go. As they did so, the woman stopped and looked directly at the boy.

"Those who oppress others shall suffer pain worse than they inflicted," she said. "When you wish to join us, young one, do so openly—as I did, once, and as my mother did before me."

When the small party had gone, and the torchlight faded, Samuel ran home. He never told his parents what he'd seen, but he lived by the river all his life. He eventually married, and once every day, when the sun went down, he walked off to the marshes, smiling at the frogs but leaving them be, continuing on to the bayou and what he had come to regard as his most sacred task.

# 1887: The Discovery

He was waiting out the storm when he found the nearly naked man.

On Sundays like this, when the sun was warm and the air clear, sixty-year-old Duncan Madison enjoyed strolling along the shores of the Hudson River. Six days each week, he ran the Park Avenue Oyster House across from Grand Central Station, as he'd done for nearly thirty-five years, ever since he left the navy. He enjoyed the work and his regular clientele, but he didn't like the choking fumes from the trains, the smell from the horse-cars lined up at the curb and waiting for fares, the clanging and clattering of the trolleys which ran along Forty-Second Street; and most of all, he hated the chatter of the out-of-towners who thought the seafood was better in Connecticut or Massachusetts or upstate or wherever they came in from.

On Sundays, Madison enjoyed packing himself a basket, leaving his room behind the restaurant, and walking west, to the Hudson River, where he'd spend the day roaming up and down its banks. There, he reflected on how much more civilized the city was when he was a child. He could almost imagine how it was a century before, two centuries before, when there were only trees and rich soil and deer.

On the warm Sunday in July, Madison had settled down on a big, flat rock overhanging the water. He'd just opened his basket when a rainstorm blew in from the Atlantic. Ducking under the rock, Madison felt like a boy again as he listened to the fat raindrops pounding overhead, and watched the choppy waters of the Hudson.

The moan brought him back to reality.

It came from the north, and he cupped his ears, listened again to make sure it wasn't the wind. When he heard it again, Madison pulled up his collar and ran into the pelting rain.

The man was lying on his back on the rocky shore. There was a wrecked rowboat several yards from him, and he was stretching his arm toward it. A few items were scattered about, including a broken keg, a tattered map, and a book.

Reaching the man's side, Madison stripped off his own coat and wrapped it around the bare figure. He had graying hair, a scraggly beard, and was deeply tanned. He was extremely emaciated, the bones of his cheeks and shoulders nearly poking through his skin.

"My . . . son . . ." the figure wheezed.

Madison took a quick look around. "There's no one else here. Are you hurt, sir?"

"Must . . . find John."

The figure tried to rise. Madison gently pushed him back and said he'd look for other survivors.

Wading into the river, he shielded his eyes with a hand and peered through the sheets of rain. He saw no one, and the current was strong enough that if he went in any further, he might be washed away. Walking nearly a quarter-mile in both directions along the riverbank, Madison came up empty-handed. He went back to the man.

"I'm sorry, but there isn't anyone here. Now, sir, don't try to move. I'm going to get help."

The man protested weakly, but didn't move.

The only one Madison knew who had a carriage was Abram Polinsky, who ran the New Washington Market where he often bought his fish. He ran all the way to Forty-Seventh Street and Broadway, the flagstones hurting his feet. The streets were deserted, and he pounded on the door of Polinsky's apartment. Five minutes later, the men were hurrying west on the ramshackle cart.

Unable to bring it to the riverbank, they left it on a ledge less than a hundred yards away, and ran down through the slackening rain.

When they reached the man, he was crawling toward the shattered boat.

"Please," he coughed when the men took hold of him, "let . . . me . . . go."

"You'll be all right if you come with us," Madison said.

As they picked him up, Polinsky said to Madison, "I've not seen a rowboat like that before. Not that shape."

"The man's English, can't you tell? He must've come in on one of the traders."

"John. John," the man said weakly.

"I'll come back and look for him," Madison promised as they carried him up the ledge to the cart. They set him in back, and while Polinsky tucked him beneath the canvas, Madison went back for his basket and the man's few belongings. When he returned, Polinsky whipped his horse to haste.

The rain had stopped, and the sun came out, the air even fresher than before. While they rode, Madison opened the water-stained book. It was a log, and he gingerly separated the pages, the ink having run across most of them. Toward the center, however, some of the writing was legible.

"Listen," Madison said. " 'February 11: icebound in the bay, crew hungry, cold.' " The rest was indecipherable, and he moved down several entries to the next unsoiled line. " 'Crew pressing to return to England, must find Northwest Passage.' "

"How old is that book?" Polinsky asked.

"I don't know, but the script is old-fashioned." He read on. " 'June 23: sailors mutinied. John and loyal men to leave *Discovery,* cast adrift, no food or arms.' And here's an entry from yesterday. 'July 10: traded last of clothing to natives for food. I fear for—'"

Madison stopped.

"Fear for what?" Polinsky pressed.

"It doesn't say. He stopped writing."

"That must be when they were caught in the storm."

"Most likely. The *Discovery*—I seem to have heard of that before."

"It's a common enough name, Duncan. Every man who comes to the market has sailed either a *Discovery* or *Enterprise* or *Something-or-Other Belle.*

Madison shook his head, then turned back to the unfortunate sea captain. And grasped Polinsky's arm so tightly that the fishmonger gasped.

"Duncan, are you out of—"

"Look! *Look!*"

Reining in the horse, Polinsky turned; his jaw slackened when he looked back.

The canvas was still stretched where he'd left it, but the man was gone.

"Lord, Duncan, where could he have gotten off?"

Madison had no idea, but they turned the cart around and retraced their course to the river. They didn't find the man, nor did they see the wreckage of his boat. Both men walked downriver for a considerable distance, looking to see if the vessel had washed away, but they saw no trace of it either ashore or in the river.

They returned to the cart, where Madison grabbed Polinsky again.

"What *now?*"

"Either we're both mad, or this is a joke."

"Why?"

He pointed to the seat: the book, map, and other items were also gone. Only Madison's basket was still there.

"It's a joke," Polinsky concluded.

"If so, it's an extraordinary one. The only footprints in the mud, Abram, are our own."

"Are you telling me none of this ever happened?" Polinsky asked as they stood looking out across the calm river.

Madison had no idea, and the men decided to go back to the Park Avenue Oyster House to open a bottle of brandy. They sat in the empty restaurant and went over everything that had happened. Suddenly Polinsky froze and stared at the wall behind Madison.

"Oh my God," he said.

Madison turned slowly, afraid of what he might see. His eyes scanned the wall and settled on the spot where Polinsky was looking.

There was a fading painting there, one of a half-dozen which had been put there by his late wife. Madison must have looked at them thousands of times without really seeing them; at least, not being *aware* of seeing them. But in the dim gaslight of the oyster house, he saw this one now.

The long, narrow ship was the *Discovery,* and the brass plaque beneath it read, "Henry Hudson's Last Voyage."

The men looked at one another.

"He was set adrift by his men," Madison said, "never to be seen again." He walked over to the painting, looked at the small, bearded figures on the deck of the ship. "Never again, until today."

Polinsky snorted. "That wasn't Henry Hudson, Duncan. Henry Hudson lived two hundred years ago."

"Then who *was* it?"

"Some other poor soul."

"A poor soul is right," Madison said, and for the remainder of his life was convinced that he had encountered the spirit of the sailor who had been shipwrecked making for warmer waters, and died on the banks of the river which bore his name.

Died—two centuries earlier.

# 1907: *Marine Corpse*

Mrs. Sutton wasn't satisfied with the official explanation—and neither was her son.

Her son was James Sutton, and he'd left their comfortable home in Portland, Oregon, to become a marine officer at the United States Naval Academy in Annapolis. On October 12, Mrs. Sutton had a totally unfounded but unshakable feeling that her boy would be visiting. She and her daughter Louise went to his bedroom and changed the linens on the bed, dusted, and made sure everything was in order. Teenage Louise was both surprised and worried by her mother's insistence that he'd be there.

However, Louise was even more surprised when her father came home early from work that day. He looked ashen and barely acknowledged her as he walked in. He went right upstairs to his wife, took her in his arms, and said, "I had a telegram at the office, from the academy. They say our son shot himself. He's dead."

Louise and her brother Dan and sister Daisy had come to the doorway, and all stood there and wept. Their mother did not. She looked at her husband, then looked beside him: there was James, dressed in his uniform, shimmering ever so slightly and looking healthier than his father.

"Mamma," the young man said, "I didn't kill myself. My hands are as clean as when I was a boy. I was murdered, Mamma. They murdered me."

Mrs. Sutton stood staring at her son while her husband hugged her and began to weep.

"Don't you see him?" she asked. "Our Jimmie is here."

"Our Jimmie is dead," her husband said.

"No, he's here, beside you! He *spoke* to me!"

Mr. Sutton made no reply, but pulled her tightly to him. Suddenly, his wife began talking again.

"He says they struck him on the back of the head, hard."

"Mamma," Louise said through her own tears, "please stop! Jimmie's not here!"

But the woman continued, "Three men surrounded him and began beating him. They knocked him down, leaned on his neck and shoulders, pushed his face against the ground. They broke his watch when they pummeled him, then stepped on his wrist to pin him on the ground, just before . . . one of them shot him."

The woman looked at her husband. She seemed disoriented, as though she'd suddenly wakened from sleep.

"He's gone, now," she said. "But he begged me to bring his killers to justice, or he will never know peace."

Mr. Sutton believed only that his wife was overwrought, and refused to go to authorities at the academy because of a vision his wife had had. However, five days later, Mrs. Sutton had another visit from her son.

She was alone in her room, resting after a sleepless night, when she heard James's voice close to her ear.

"Mamma," he said.

She opened her eyes and stared at him standing stiffly beside her.

"They kicked me, kept kicking my forehead until it was covered with blood, and the left side of my jaw was swollen. Then they covered my head with a cloth to conceal what they had done. It hurt so, Mamma. Please don't let them get away with it. Please bring them to justice."

James vanished when she reached out to touch him, and Mrs. Sutton was more convinced than before that she had not imagined his visit. If it were her own mind inventing the visitations, why would she create descriptions of her son's face and condition, instead of reliving pleasant memories?

She tried to tell herself that she had never experienced any horror like losing a child, and her mind was reacting in kind. Yet, after a short nap, she was awakened by a wheezing sound. She looked up to see her son standing beside her, his face battered nearly beyond recognition. Blood ran thickly down his cheeks and onto his uniform, his flesh was ringed with dark, blue bruises, and his jaw was lopsided, bone straining against skin on the left side.

"Don't believe what they tell you," he said through bloodied lips. "I did not take my life. They did it. They killed me."

Mrs. Sutton screamed for her husband. As a result of this latest vision, she neither slept nor ate for days. She was too weak to attend the memorial services at Arlington National Cemetery, and Louise went alone. However, immediately upon her daughter's return, Mrs. Sutton showed renewed strength and asked urgently to see James's belongings.

Louise handed her the suitcase. Tossing clothing and other items aside, Mrs. Sutton triumphantly produced her son's watch and held it up for the family to see: the crystal was shattered.

"You see!" she cackled. "It's just as he said, my boy *was* murdered! And he was here to tell me that!"

By this time, documents recounting the inquest into James's death had arrived. Mr. Sutton read them, and then his own suspicions grew. According to the official inquiry, James had gone to a dance with some friends. They drank too much, and on the way back to the academy began to argue about a girl they'd met. Shoving followed, and James was so drunk and angry that he vowed to kill two of his companions. When he reached his room, he gathered his pistol and ammunition and went after the others. However, they had reported his threats to the authorities, and when the military police arrived to arrest him, he opened fire—on himself.

Mr. Sutton knew that his son was neither violent nor a heavy drinker. He contacted academy authorities, but they insisted that their doctors, under oath, had said there were no disfiguring marks on the boy, apart from the gunshot wound.

Stymied, Mr. Sutton saw no choice but to let the case be, until, that is, his wife said their son appeared to her yet again.

It was the middle of the night, and she awoke to see James, once more unblemished, kneeling beside her bed. In his hands was a picture of his class, which she kept framed on her bureau.

He pointed to a face. "Utley killed me, and they kept me in his basement while the authorities decided what to do. Decided how to blame me to keep the honor of the academy unstained."

The picture fell to the floor and shattered, waking Mr. Sutton. He looked over at his wife, who told him through her tears what James had said. Mr. Sutton looked at the broken picture frame. A light sleeper, he knew he'd have awakened if his wife had climbed from bed to get the picture. He believed her and, together, they made the most difficult decision of their life: to have James's body disinterred and examined by doctors outside the military.

This was done, and the findings corroborated everything Mrs. Sutton had claimed. Not only had James been badly beaten, but the angle of the gunshot wound was such that it could not have been self-inflicted.

Everyone involved in the original inquest was relieved of their duties, and an order was given to arrest the men who had taken part in the beating. All were brought in, save for Utley, who had run away. Despite an exhaustive search, he was never found.

Though James's name was cleared, his ghost did not vanish immediately. Sometimes, Mrs. Sutton saw him in his room, just standing and staring at this memento or that; sometimes he would look on while the family was at dinner.

But every time he appeared, he was not quite as clear as the time before, and finally, on the third anniversary of his death, he stopped appearing altogether.

Yet Mrs. Sutton knew he was still there, with her, and it's unlikely that anyone was ever as glad that there are such things as ghosts.

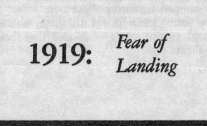

# 1919:  *Fear of Landing*

Ever since he was seven, when the Wright brothers made their historic flight at nearby Kitty Hawk, Tucker Lee wanted to fly.

Growing up in Grandy, North Carolina, the son of a blacksmith, Lee joined the army in 1914. He learned to repair planes, then to fly them, and fought in Europe in World War I. Unfortunately, he never saw real combat. He was given only a sluggish Hanriot and was only responsible for directing artillery fire. Yet that didn't stop him from being a target, and on his tenth flight his plane was riddled with gunfire from a Fokker triplane. Managing to crash-land, Lee suffered a severe concussion, and after a stay in a French hospital, he was sent home. Working on so many aircraft and surviving a crash only fueled Lee's love of airplanes.

In 1918, shortly after the war's end, he learned of an English newspaper which was offering 10,000 pounds to any aviator who flew nonstop across the Atlantic Ocean. Determined to win that prize, Lee acquired a battlescarred Martinsyde. Working in his father's smithie by day, he refurbished the biplane at night, repairing and streamlining it, finding ways to increase its fuel efficiency.

After several promising flights over land, Lee decided it was time to test his aircraft over the open sea. Plotting a course which would carry him east over the Atlantic, southwest to Pamlico Sound, and north to Albemarle Sound and back to Grandy, he set out on a chilly morning in January of 1919.

Quickly reaching 120 miles per hour, which had been top speed for the Martinsyde, he waited until he was over the ocean before pushing it to 150 miles per hour. His improvements worked and the plane sliced gracefully through the clear skies. On the southwest leg of the journey, however, his engine began to smoke and burn. Whether it was the purer fuel or the greater oxygen mix didn't matter just then; the important thing was to get back to the mainland.

He swung due west, but the plane nosed down and lost altitude quickly. Waves of slate-gray smoke obscured Lee's view. He didn't fight to stay aloft, concentrating as best he could on keeping the plane steady, hoping that when he could see *something,* he'd have enough fuel to attempt a landing. Suddenly, there was a staccato rapping against his landing gear, then against the undercarriage, and finally the propeller of the Martinsyde was nipping at the treetops. The plane hit them a moment later and flipped over, somersaulting twice before coming to rest, upside down in the trees.

Choking on the smoke, and battered from the crash landing, Lee looked down. The ground was about twenty feet below, but if he stayed up here he knew he might burn to death. Undoing his harness, he held onto it so he was hanging straight down from the cockpit. Then he let go and dropped through the trees, hitting the ground hard.

When he awoke, it was evening. There was a chill in the air, and a faint orange glow to his right. He tried to prop himself on an elbow, but pain shot through his forehead and chest. He fell back. When he opened his eyes again, a young woman was looking down at him. She was smiling, but her eyes were sad; her fair skin was dirty, her cheeks hollow, and strands of blond hair tumbled haphazardly from beneath her bonnet.

"How do you feel?" she asked. She had an English accent, like several of the nurses he had met overseas.

"I've felt better, thank you," he said, wincing. He was sure he'd broken some ribs and aggravated his old head wound. "My name's Tucker Lee."

"I'm Victoria," the woman said. "My husband wanted to speak with you, but he went with the others, looking for your ship."

"They'll find it in some trees," he said. "My engine started to burn, but you know what they say. Any landing you can walk away from . . ."

The woman seemed puzzled. "I'm not sure I understand. If you were shipwrecked—"

"Not shipwrecked. I crash-landed."

"Well, the important thing is, were you carrying supplies?"

He looked at her strangely. "Supplies? For what?"

"For us. For anyone, really. It means our survival."

"Now *I* don't understand," he said, but a child had called out and the woman turned away. Lee lay back, touched his head and chest. The woman had opened his flight jacket and cleaned his wounds, and someone had tied a tree branch to his leg using vines; it was numb, and he knew he must have broken it jumping from the cockpit.

Since every movement caused pain, he simply lay there and thought about what she'd asked him.

Where could he have landed that supplies were so important that people were going to die without them? He rolled his head to one side and squinted into the darkness.

He was at the edge of a forest just beside a beach; there were tree stumps all around, and nearly a dozen bundles lined up along the shore, as though waiting to be loaded. Victoria was seeing to a child no older than three, the two of them sitting on a stump beside a dying campfire. There was another woman there, lying on the sands, coughing. She did not sound well.

Now that he saw Victoria's full figure, Lee was more confused than before. She wasn't dressed like anyone he'd ever seen. She wore a long, dirty, brown dress and blouse, with a white collar and ragged white sleeves. Her feet were wrapped in pelts, and around her shoulders was a fur wrap which looked like bearskin. It struck him that the only place he'd ever seen a costume like that was in a picture book. A book about the colonization of America.

His head was throbbing. This had to be a mirage of some kind, what Foreign Legionnaires he'd met in France had reported seeing in the desert.

After a few minutes, three men came down the beach. They were dressed in clothing as alien as Victoria's. One man bent beside the ailing woman and put a water pouch to her lips, another embraced Victoria, and a third sat down heavily, by himself. He seemed to be crying. As Lee looked at him, he thought he saw a cross listing in the sands.

"There is no ship," said the one who held Victoria, "our hope was ill-placed. We have no choice but to take the raft and try for the continent at sunrise."

Victoria nodded, then said gamely, "The Croatoan will help us. If we can but reach shore, they will help us all."

*The Croatoan?* Lee thought. *Indians? What's going on?*

The man released Victoria, then looked at Lee. "Did he tell you anything?"

"He is feverish. His words make no sense."

"We'll take him," he said. "If he survives, perhaps he can tell us where his boat landed."

Lee told himself this simply couldn't be. It was possible he was further south than he thought, and had gone down on Roanoke Island. But these people could not be what they appeared to be: the settlers left by Walter Raleigh in 1587. He had to be delirious.

Lee tried to get up, to call to the man, but the pressure on his chest caused him to gasp and fall back. Dark red circles swirled before his eyes, and after a moment of fighting the awful pain, he blacked out.

The next thing Lee knew, someone was shaking him by the shoulder. He opened his eyes, then shut them quickly to block out the blinding sunlight.

"Fella, you alive?"

Lee nodded weakly.

"Y'barely look it. What happened?"

"Plane wreck," was all he could manage.

"Oh yeah? Well, where's yer plane?"

Lee opened his eyes a crack. There was a man standing above him. He was grizzled, his suit fancy but old, like a travelling preacher, but he was definitely a man of the modern day.

With effort, the flier stretched out his arm and indicated for the man to help him sit up. His chest hurt, though his head felt better than it had the night before.

"My plane," Lee repeated, and looked around. He was on a beach on the mainland; Roanoke Island was dimly visible to his right, maybe three miles across the sound. "I hit treetops," he muttered, "flipped over."

"Not here, y'didn't," the man said. "No trees here."

Lee looked to his left. The man was right. There was nothing but beach and dune for at least a half-mile. He had to have crash-landed on Roanoke.

The man helped Lee into his buggy and brought him to a doctor in Buffalo City.

For the next few weeks, Lee wondered about what had really happened to him. His folks and everyone else said that he had to have gone down at sea and swum ashore, but he knew he'd hit trees. They said he must have imagined that. And the strange people in funny clothes.

Finally, though, he convinced a friend to lend him a sailboat so he could go out to the island.

There, after searching for nearly a day, he found the wreckage of his plane. He knew then that he owed his survival to people long dead. Had the guardian ghosts not brought him to the mainland with them, he wouldn't have been found for days, possibly weeks, and might well have died.

The starving colonists may have left Roanoke Island in 1591 and vanished from the pages of history, but only Tucker Lee knew for certain that they didn't vanish *completely.*

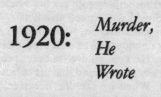

# 1920: Murder, He Wrote

Alonzo Allan and his lifelong friend Cole Farrell were co-owners of a ranch in Montana, a spread coveted by the land-hungry Faye Dow.

Dow wasn't above using any tactic, including murder, to get Allan and Farrell out of the way. But he wanted to keep himself and his men from getting their hands dirty and so came up with a plan to try first. If that failed, *then* he'd kill the men.

Riding to the ranch one afternoon, Dow told Allan that Farrell had been seen in town the night before with Allan's fiancee, Jennie Michaels.

Allan laughed at the charge, said that Farrell was on the range, looking at new grazing lands, and wouldn't be back until the following morning.

Dow shook his head.

"I don't like Farrell," he said, "I don't think I've ever made a secret of that. But I like you. And frankly, Alonzo,

I'd rather have just you an' your lady as neighbors than that stiff-necked cuss." He shrugged. "Ignore what I'm about to say if you want, but ask yourself what reason I'd have to lie. And ask your girl something too: ask her where she got that pretty gold necklace I saw Farrell give her."

With a look of sheer disgust, Allan told his visitor to go. Riding off, Dow dismounted to wait atop a bluff overlooking the property. He kept an eye on the rancher. He knew Allan was extremely jealous, and that his curiosity would get the best of him. When he saw the necklace, he wouldn't believe what Jennie would tell him, that a stranger had left it for her. He'd believe that Farrell had given it to her, just as Dow had said. Then nothing would keep him from killing his partner.

And nothing would stop the county from hanging Allan for the crime. It would be worth the cost of a necklace to Dow.

Sure enough, before a half-hour had passed, Allan had saddled his gray Appaloosa and galloped into town. He went directly to the newspaper where his fiancee worked as a secretary. She smiled broadly, surprised to see him. Pointing to the necklace, Allan demanded to know where she'd got it; she said the box had been left for her—from him, she'd thought—and, as Dow had anticipated, Allan didn't believe her. Running from the office, the rancher jumped back on his horse and rode to the range.

Farrell was an expert shot, so rather than face him in the open, Allan decided to wait for him behind a bend. He'd be coming through sometime after midnight, at which point Allan would gun him down.

He waited, sitting behind a boulder, barely feeling the chill when the sun set. He was warmed by his anger, by the sense of betrayal he felt. He debated about whether to give Farrell a chance to explain, then decided against it. He'd only lie, the way his fiancee had done.

Not long after midnight, when a sharp crescent moon was high overhead, Allan heard hoofbeats. He unholstered his revolver and crouched behind the rock, wanting to wait until his quarry was closer.

Suddenly, the hoofbeats stopped. Allan remained pressed

against the stone, wondering what was wrong. Farrell couldn't know he was here. He'd hidden his horse in a cave over a mile back, and had practically held his damn breath so it wouldn't show in the cold night air.

It had to be something else. Slowly, Allan rose and looked over the top of the boulder.

Much to his surprise, the newcomer wasn't Farrell. It was a lone steer, but one larger than any Allan had ever seen. Black and evil-looking, it had horns almost as thick as a big man's arms; white breath (or was it smoke?) rose from the animal's nostrils as it stood there. However, Allan got the biggest jolt when the steer clopped forward and he could see its side.

The word *Murder* was branded there, the letters red, as though the branding iron had been pressed there within the hour. The creature turned toward where Allan was standing, and lowered its head.

The boulder was too steep to climb, and there was nowhere to run. When the animal snorted and charged, Allan had no choice but to stand his ground and fire repeatedly.

Six bullets struck the animal in the head, and as Allan reloaded, the beast continued to charge, though at the same time it grew and spread and finally just vanished.

As Allan stood there, he heard hoofbeats behind him. He turned as Dow came riding up. The rancher had his own gun unholstered.

"Allan, I heard shots! Are you all right?"

The rancher looked at him. What was Dow doing out here?

Just then, Farrell came riding from the direction the steer had come. He was approaching at a gallop, also in response to the shots.

Dow stopped and looked at the oncoming figure. There was a strange look on his face. And Allan suddenly understood.

"You did this," Allan said to Dow. "You gave Jennie the necklace and then lied to me, knowing I'd come after Farrell. Then you planned to take me in."

"That's ridiculous!" Dow exclaimed.

"Then what are you doing out here?"

"Looking for stray cattle."

"Alone? At night?"

Dow began backing away as Farrell rode up. Suddenly, Dow fired at Allan; the rancher went down, with a bullet in his side, but before Dow could shoot at Farrell, the wounded Allan had drawn, fired six more shots, and stitched Dow to the boulder.

Farrell brought his wounded partner and Dow's body back to town, where as soon as he was fit enough, Allan was put on trial for the rancher's murder.

Against the advice of his attorney, Allan told about why he had fired: about the steer he'd seen. The court clearly didn't believe that part of the testimony, but accepted the rest, about Dow framing Farrell and then shooting first. Allan was acquitted.

As he left the courtroom with Farrell and Jennie, a thin, old man with deep wrinkles and pale eyes came up to them. The three recognized him as having been in the courtroom throughout the week-long trial.

"You saw Murder," the old man said to Allan.

"Pardon?"

"For thirty years I been followin' him," the man said, "seein' that the job got done."

"What job?" Allan demanded.

The man said, "The job Zachary Spencer bid it to do. When Zachary and his brother Gilbert argued over who owned the prize longhorn, it ended with Zachary gunning his brother down—and then feelin' such remorse that he ordered me to brand the steer with the name Murder and set him free. Zachary said, 'I pray to God Almighty that he haunts the plains forever, stopping others from doing what I have done.' And then put the barrel of his gun in his mouth and pulled the trigger.

"That was in Brewster County, Texas. A few weeks later, I heard from a rustler that a steer like the one I cut loose was seen in the Dakotas. Then someone swore they'd seen him back in Texas. He seemed to appear everywhere over the years, always where brothers or a father and son or friends like you were about to turn on one another. And each time, it didn't happen 'cause Murder stopped them by scarin' them off, carryin' out Zachary's will."

The old man apologized to Jennie for having told such a gruesome story, then left. Farrell had a dubious look on his face, and Jennie hugged Allan's arm with fear. But Allan was composed. Composed and grateful that Murder had done its job.

# 1921: The Black Cat's Return

When he accepted the position as captain of the schooner *Nancy Hanks,* Thomas Dorn had no idea it was cursed. And when he found out, he wasn't particularly impressed: a seasoned seaman, he was accustomed to sailors' superstitions.

In fact, Dorn's family had produced three generations of ship's officers, and one of the things which Dorn loved about the sea was its wealth of folklore. When he was a boy, his father and grandfather were always telling him tales of the sea serpent in Lake Champlain, of the mermaids which sometimes frolicked off the coast of Maine, of the ghosts of dead sailors of the Revolution, the War of 1812, and the Civil War. There were sailors who walked on the water or prowled the shores, who trailed water and seaweed behind them as they guarded spots where treasure was buried or where their ships had been sunk.

Still, this story was unique. It was the first time Captain Dorn had heard of a ship being haunted by an animal.

It was the ship's cook, rangy, black-haired Liam, who told him the story.

Ten years before, when the *Nancy Hanks* was on its maiden voyage, one of the sailors had found a black cat in the hold. Fearing that the animal would bring the ship bad luck, he lured the cat to him with cheese, grabbed it, carried it to the deck, and tossed it overboard.

He stood there and watched, content, as the cat bobbed for a moment before vanishing.

That same night, the helmsman came running below, screaming that there was a pale white cat perched atop the wheel, and that he couldn't control their course. Laughter and disbelief greeted his claim, but as a handful of curious sailors filed on deck, the ship struck a reef. It was months before the vessel could be made seaworthy again. No cat was ever found onboard.

Captain Dorn suggested that maybe the helmsman had been drinking, as the breed was known to do when alone on deck. Liam insisted that that was not the case, that the drowned cat had returned to wreak vengeance upon the *Nancy Hanks*.

Liam was the only one of the previous crewmembers who signed aboard for the new voyage.

The ship was making a run from New Orleans to New York. It left early on the morning of March 20, and all went well for the first day. The winds were strong and steady, the seas relatively calm, the crew efficient.

At sunset, however, the seas changed.

A squall came up suddenly from out of the southeast, battering the vessel relentlessly. Several times the *Nancy Hanks* heeled severely, hanging precariously on its side and threatening to go over.

One sailor swore he saw a white light atop the masts. Most of the men thought it was St. Elmo's fire. Captain Dorn was inclined to agree. But Liam knew they were wrong. He knew it was the cat.

The second day of the journey passed without incident. That night, however, Captain Dorn was awakened by loud scuffing sounds forward of his cabin, in the galley. He went out to investigate.

Liam was bent over, his back to the door, his head moving from side to side. He appeared to be looking for something.

There was a bucket in his hands.

"Liam?"

The cook spun quickly, and liquid splashed from the pail. He wore a wild, disheveled look.

"Captain! I didn't hear you! I . . . I was just cleaning."

"At two in the morning?" The captain came closer, and smelled the odor which permeated the galley. "Kerosene. What are you doing with that?"

"Sir, it's . . . it's the *cat*, Captain. I *saw* him."

Dorn reached for the bucket. "Give me that, Liam. You don't know what you're saying."

"I *do!* It *was* the cat. He came to me, grinning. I followed him. He wants to destroy us all. I must *burn* him! I read about that when I was ashore in a book about spirits. That's the only way to destroy a demon!"

"Liam—"

"Captain, I'm the only one can do it. *I* was the sailor that threw him overboard. I've been watching for him."

"There's no cat."

"I tell you, there *is!*"

Backing away, the cook suddenly dropped the bucket and grabbed the matches from beside the stove.

"You've got to let me burn him! You must!"

"You'll destroy the ship, Liam."

"You can take the lifeboats. If I don't stop him, he'll kill us all! He exists to destroy this ship!"

Liam struck one of the matches. The captain held out both hands and told him to stay calm. The cook had reached a corner, between the small stove and sink.

So quickly that the captain wasn't sure what he'd seen, there was a white flash between them and what sounded like a snarl. The match flew from Liam's hand, and moments later, a wall of flame erupted between them. Captain Dorn reached for the cook, but was unable to get through the flames. Nor could he reach the sink to pump water. Engulfed in flame, Liam struggled briefly and then was still.

Running to the crew's quarters, Dorn yelled for the men to abandon ship.

The schooner's four lifeboats were quickly lowered, Captain Dorn waiting until everyone was safely over the side before joining them.

As they rowed away, he looked back at the ship. The fire had spread quickly, and flames were already bursting through the deck. They were licking at the three tall masts, sending flecks of burning sail into the night sky.

Along with something else.

They heard a cry like nothing the captain had ever heard at sea. One which rose above the flame and echoed across the waters. The high, earsplitting wail . . . of a cat.

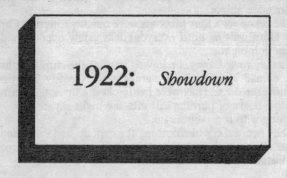

# 1922: *Showdown*

It was a small inn along the Pecos River just southeast of Fort Sumner, and the newlyweds stopped for the night.

Police officer Jonathan Walker and his wife Gail had been married that morning in Santa Rosa, and were driving to Clovis to visit a friend with whom Jonathan had served in the Great War. Rather than drive straight through, they decided to rest and get a leisurely start in the morning.

Leaving their seven-year-old, four-seat Fergus parked beside the large but empty inn, they signed in and ordered dinner in the quaint dining room. Throughout the meal, Jonathan had the same feeling he often had when he patrolled in Santa Rosa, that someone was watching him. But he knew that couldn't be true; the only one watching him was Gail, and he concentrated on being as attentive as he could to his new bride.

After retiring to their room, Jonathan lay in the soft bed, dressed in his pajamas, waiting for his wife to finish with her toilet. He didn't mind waiting. They'd waited for seven months; another few minutes wouldn't matter. If anything, his anticipation grew keener.

Suddenly, the little noises in the bathroom stopped. After a moment, Jonathan called to his wife.

"Gail, is everything all right?"

It took her a long moment to reply. "Jonathan—come here."

Leaping from the bed, Jonathan crossed the small room and pulled open the door.

Gail was facing him, her hands across her mouth, her eyes on the floor, by his feet. He looked down. There were several drops of blood on the tiles.

"Are you all right?" Jonathan asked.

"It's not mine," she said. "It just . . . appeared."

Jonathan went over to her, looked at her arms and legs. "You must have nicked yourself somewhere, darling."

She shook her head. "I heard breathing, and when I turned, the blood was there."

Jonathan looked up at the ceiling. There was no leak there, and, wiping away the spots on the floor, he waited to see if it had seeped through the tile. Neither seemed possible and, pulling on his trousers, he went out to get the proprietor.

An accommodating old woman, she had no explanation for the blood. However, she did take Gail aside and discreetly asked if she might need any "feminine items." Gail assured her that that wasn't the case.

The woman happened to glance at the luggage stand, where the couple's suitcase was open. Jonathan's police revolver sat amidst the clothing, and she looked at it for a long moment.

"I don't keep guns here."

Jonathan said, "I'm a policeman. I take target practice when I can."

The woman seemed to want to say something, but, as though deciding against it, left the room in a hurry.

"She was a big help," Gail said, returning to the bathroom and finishing up with the door open. When she finished, she hurried into bed. Under the covers and in her husband's arms, she felt much better.

Until something scraped along the bathroom floor.

Jonathan heard it, too, and was out of bed and in the bathroom even before Gail had sat up. He switched on the light.

"This is crazy," he said, looking in the empty room. He bent and looked along the molding and inside the bathtub. "It must be an animal, maybe a mouse."

Gail nodded. And then she screamed.

Jonathan turned, and for a flashing moment he thought he saw a figure standing between them. He hurried to the spot where it had been standing. There were drops of blood on the floor.

"That was no animal," he said. He touched the drops and rubbed some of the blood between his thumb and index finger. "And this *is* blood."

"Jonathan!"

He looked at her, then followed her arm, which was pointing toward the door.

There *was* someone standing there; they could hear strained breath, see drops of blood splashing on the wooden floor.

"What *is* it?" Gail shrieked.

Jonathan didn't know what to say. He just stood there looking for a point of origin as the breathing grew faint and then vanished. The blood remained, a dark blotch on the floor, and then it, too, disappeared.

"I'm going to see that old lady again," he said. "She *knows* something."

"I'm coming with you," Gail said, pulling on a robe; but something grabbed the garment by the collar and pulled the woman back. She fell onto the bed, shrieking, and pushed herself up. There were spots of blood on the sheets, and more appeared like drops of rain.

Suddenly, blood began falling onto her lap and dripping on her arms. Jonathan launched himself at her, felt around the bed, but encountered nothing. He turned, saw the blood form a trail toward the front door. Only this time, it didn't stop. The air itself seemed to bleed until a shape appeared. It was white and hazy, like the figure they'd seen before, but now it didn't disappear. It rippled, as though waves were passing over it, and took on more and more substance with each moment.

"Jonathan, what *is* it?"

He had no idea what to say. More blood was dripping, pouring between what looked like fingers splayed across a man's chest. Now they clearly saw the figure of a young man standing in front of them. He was unkempt, breathing heavily, listing to one side. He was dressed in clothing from the previous century; there was a gun in his free hand, and it was pointing toward them.

Jonathan moved between the apparition and his wife. "What do you want?"

The figure, now solid, moved toward the luggage stand, turned his head slowly, and looked into the valise.

"Your gun," Gail said. "The old woman said she didn't keep them."

"With good reason."

The intruder's eyes turned from the weapon to the couple. There was a strange look in its eyes, as though it were confused. Jonathan took that as a sign that it was a good time to go, and, still using his body to shield his wife, they started slowly toward the door. Then, far more quickly than it had appeared, the figure vanished. When it did, Jonathan jumped for the door, pulling Gail behind him.

The couple ran down the corridor and pounded the bell at the registration desk. The woman emerged from a back room, and Jonathan demanded to know what was happening.

"He wouldn't hurt you, you know."

Jonathan glowered at her. "Then you *know* what this is about?"

She moved her shoulders noncommittally. "Guns make him nervous, but he's never hurt anyone."

*"Who* hasn't?"

"William. William Bonney."

Jonathan stared at her. "Bonney? Billy the Kid?"

She nodded. "Shot not far from here by Sheriff Pat Garrett."

"But that was at least forty years ago!"

"Forty-two. The only people who have seen him since

then are people who have a gun. They've never stayed. It's said that Bonney is looking for Garrett."

Gail was shaking her head. "You don't know what you're saying!" She grabbed her husband's arm. "We're leaving, Jonathan. *Now.*"

He nodded, and left her in the lobby while he went back to the room and closed his suitcase.

The gun wasn't there.

He looked through the clothing, then around the room.

The figure was standing in a darkened corner, its gun pointed at him. Jonathan's own gun lay on the floor, between the wraith's feet. It was completely covered with blood.

"My name is Jonathan Walker," he said softly. "I mean you no harm."

The apparition bent slightly with pain. Its hand was red with blood.

"The man you want is dead. You shouldn't be here. You can't change anything."

Jonathan couldn't believe he was standing there, trying to reason with a dead man. *Fearing* a dead man. It occurred to him, then, that the man would not shoot him, unarmed, as he'd been shot. Turning his back, Jonathan closed the suitcase slowly.

He felt the ghost's eyes upon him, as he had before, in the dining room. He could hear the gentle sound of the blood striking the floor and knew, without looking, that the creature was beside him.

He refused to look. Hefting the suitcase from the stand, he kept his eyes downturned as he walked to the door.

Taking his wife's hand, Jonathan led her silently to the car. They drove on to Clovis that night.

Two years later, Jonathan learned that a sheriff visiting the inn had died from a gunshot wound. The bullet had come from his own gun, and his death was declared a suicide.

But Jonathan knew better. Jonathan knew that the man had seen what he himself had seen, had probably reached for his gun, and was killed.

Killed in the fair fight which Bonney had been denied in life.

# 1932: *The Uninterred*

It's said that the woods of northern Michigan are the best hunting grounds in the nation. The French trappers who lived there made that claim as far back as the middle of the seventeenth century; in this century, people who live there or visit can go from Hiawatha National Forest in the east to Porcupine Mountains State Park in the west and never be disappointed by the scenery or the game, which ranges from partridge and rabbit to deer.

During the Depression, young Allan Jones lived with his parents in a small house in the middle of a pine forest. He walked, each morning, to the one-room schoolhouse which was attended by fourteen other children. He was accompanied by his father Sam, who also happened to be the teacher. In the afternoons, when Allan was finished with his homework and had completed his chores, he would go out with his .22 and hunt rabbits, pretending they were wolverines.

For several days during the late winter, when rainfall had

been heavy, he hadn't been able to go into his beloved woods, where the muck was thick. Finally, though, several days of light snowfall froze the ground and he was able to hunt again.

There had been a light snowfall while he was at school, and enough remained on the ground so that the animal tracks were easy to follow. However, when he was well into the woods, Allan also saw tracks he couldn't identify: big furry blotches, slightly larger than a man's foot. They followed the path of the rabbit tracks, though the big tracks overlapped the rabbit prints in spots. Whatever it was, it had been through recently. Allan continued on, despite the gnawing fear that the tracks might be those of a bear or a monster.

Eventually, they came to a shallow ravine in a rutted and sloping section of the woods he hadn't visited for some time before the rains. In the fading light, the boy could just barely make out a man lying twenty feet down, at the bottom. He was dressed in tattered furs, from head to toe, which accounted for the strange footprints. Two stacks of pelts lay beside him.

"Hey, mister!" Allan yelled. "Are you hurt?"

A grizzled face turned slowly upward. *"S'il vous . . . plaît . . . aidez . . . moi . . ."*

"You ate what?"

*"Ma jambe,"* he rasped.

"I can't make out what you're saying," the boy shouted down. "But if you stay put, I'll go and get my dad."

Running back through the woods, Allan returned with the elder Jones, a lantern, a blanket, and rope. By the time they arrived, the man was unconscious.

Sam rappeled down, followed by his son, and they bundled the figure in the blanket. His eyes were dark, and patches of skin showed through his thinning beard. He wasn't young, but he surely wasn't as old as he looked.

"He smells," Allan remarked.

His father hushed him, then went to get a branch to use as a·splint.

"What do you think happened, Dad?"

"He must have slipped and fell." He glanced at the two

bundles of pelts. "I can't imagine where he was going with these."

As they bound the man's leg, he woke up. The man spoke only French, however, and wasn't able to explain very much to Allan or his father.

"All I can understand is his name, which is Robert Marquette. He must be from Canada."

"He doesn't have any papers on him," Allan said, patting his sides. "What are we going to do?"

"Take him home, then drive to town. Jack at the general store speaks some French. Maybe he can help us help Mr. Marquette."

When they were finished, Sam rigged a sling under the man's arms and, climbing from the ravine, pulled him up slowly. With a shoulder under each of his arms, the two helped the dazed man through the woods. Betty Jones had broth ready, and after feeding him, they laid the man before the fireplace and let him rest.

"He looks like something from a storybook," Allan said.

"He does at that," said Betty. "Just like a trapper from the old days."

"From the very old days," Sam said. "The French trappers who came this way from Canada wore clothes stitched together from pelts like this. They'd stay here a while, hunting, then sell what they'd made at stops along the lakes."

"Why don't we just let him sleep," Betty said, "and try to talk to him in the morning?"

Sam agreed, and the family went to the kitchen for dinner.

Allan turned in but couldn't sleep, wondering about the man from the ravine. Waiting until his parents had shut off the light, he threw off his covers and crept quietly into the living room.

The figure was still by the dying fire. Allan proceeded on his hands and knees so the floorboards wouldn't creak. He approached slowly, though he grew somewhat alarmed and sped up when he didn't hear the man breathing.

Suddenly, the man's head turned toward him, and Allan stopped. Waited.

The face was smiling. Allan smiled back.

*"Merci,"* the man said softly, and then the face vanished —along with the rest of Robert Marquette.

Allan screamed.

Sam came running out, but soon dismissed his son's claim that he'd simply disappeared. He pulled on his trousers and coat and, followed by his son, went out into the night to look for the trapper.

The lantern swinging in front of them, the two hurried deeper and deeper into the woods. The snow was gone and there were no tracks, so they headed in the direction of the ravine, calling the man's name.

He didn't answer. When they reached the place where Allan had found him, they understood why.

At the bottom of the ravine lay the remnants of a newly exposed skeleton—a few arm and leg bones, ribs, and the skull. There was the residue of clothing, eaten through by maggots; the stacks of pelts, too, were nearly rotted away.

Sam put a comforting arm around his son and wondered aloud if some three centuries ago, a trapper named Robert Marquette hadn't fallen into the ravine and died there.

The next day, the Jones men went back into the ravine to dig a grave, at long last putting to rest the remains of a man whose long-stifled cry for help had finally been heard.

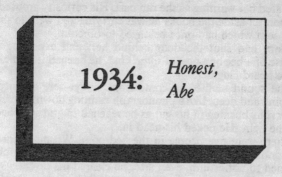

# 1934: *Honest, Abe*

Mary Eben had heard the stories about the ghost of Abraham Lincoln.

Presidents and White House employees had seen the former president roaming the residential quarters for nearly seventy years. Some were amused, some terrified, but the president never stayed for more than a few moments.

Until tonight.

There was a state banquet being held downstairs, and the secretary was in a small upstairs office, organizing some paperwork.

A creaking on the bed in an adjoining room attracted her attention. Entering cautiously, she saw the sixteenth president sitting on the bed, calmly pulling on his boots. Stopping, he looked over at her and smiled.

Mary ran from the room. Encountering domestic Wilson Graves as she scurried away, she told him to stay away from the bedroom. The elderly man asked why, but she just repeated her warning as she ran past. His curiosity aroused, Wilson set aside the books he was carrying and went to the bedroom which had once belonged to Lincoln.

Mary had shut the door behind her, and expecting a mouse or a bee or a pest of some kind, he opened it a crack.

He heard laughter.

The sound seemed to come from everywhere at once, echoing and deep, like a phonograph running down. He felt a nervous burning in his gut as he reached in and switched on the light. He poked his head in.

There were five people in the bedroom. Wilson opened the door further and took a step in. None of the people seemed to notice him, even after he cleared his throat.

They were speaking in low, resonant whispers he could barely hear, let alone understand. He looked at them for a moment. There were an extremely old man and woman seated on the edge of the bed, and three men standing around them; these men were elderly, but not so old as the couple.

Wilson looked closely at the old man on the bed. He looked familiar. He had thinning white hair and a white beard, and there was a mole on the right side of his face. He was lanky and tall and dressed in a housecoat of some kind. The woman was obese and wore her gray hair in a bun. She was dressed in a red velvet dress with bell sleeves.

He caught names as they were spoken. Willie. Edward. Tad. Mother.

Abraham.

The domestic looked at the old man on the bed. Abraham? Abraham *Lincoln?* Christ Lord, yes. It *looked* like the president, but not as he appeared in any of the photographs or portraits Wilson had seen.

Wilson shook his head. *What was he thinking?* The man had been dead since 1865.

Wilson stepped closer, wincing as his shoes squeaked. But he stopped only when Abraham looked at him. The elderly man stared at him for a moment, and then smiled slightly. The others stopped talking and turned. They did not smile.

Even when he'd braved enemy fire in the Spanish-American War, Wilson had never experienced horror such as he felt at that moment. Though these people were frail, and there was nothing malevolent about them, there was something unnatural in their voices, in the slowness of their movements. They were not real. The only question was, were they the product of his own imagination, or were they ghosts?

Willie. Edward. Tad. Those were the names of three of the four Lincoln children. Robert Lincoln had died just a few years before, at the age of eighty-three; if this were a reunion of some kind, why wasn't he here?

Wilson rubbed his eyes, but the figures didn't go away. He finally found the nerve to speak, though it took several swallows before he could clear his throat.

"Mr. P-President?"

The old man nodded once.

"Mrs. Lincoln?"

The woman looked at her husband, then down. She had a reputation for being aloof.

Wilson felt he should explain his presence, or excuse himself, but his throat had frozen up again. He simply stood and stared.

The age of these people; it made no sense. The boys had all died young, the president had been murdered, and Mrs. Lincoln had died in middle age, her mind and constitution weakened by the death of her husband and three sons.

Yet these people were old, each of an age they might have achieved had they not been stricken with youthful disease or madness or an assassin's bullet.

And it hit him, then. Is *that* what these were? The shades of a world less cruel and unjust?

"Can . . . can I get you anything?" Wilson managed to say, but even as he asked, his nerve had failed and he was backing toward the door. Abraham smiled again, but said nothing. Wilson slipped out the door and stole a look behind him—he didn't want to go bumping into William Seward or Andrew Johnson or God knew who else—and with one last glance at the family, shut the door.

And jumped as Mary Eben touched his shoulder.

She asked if he'd seen anything. He told her exactly what he saw in the bedroom, and shivering, she admitted that she'd seen Lincoln too. She asked Wilson what they should do.

He started down the hall, and picked up the books he'd left on a small table.

"We should leave them alone," he said. "That, I believe, is all they want. And it is, most definitely, what *I* want."

(Note: The ghost of Abraham Lincoln has been seen regularly at the White House over the years. Theodore Roosevelt reported, "I see Lincoln . . . in different rooms and halls." Like Eben and Wilson, Sir Winston Churchill saw Lincoln in the president's former chamber, and thereafter slept in another bedroom. The ghost also appeared to the Netherlands' Queen Wilhelmina, who—understandably—fainted when she answered the door to her room and saw Lincoln standing there. John Kenney, a bodyguard to Benjamin Harrison, was so terrified by the ghost of the former president that he asked a medium to inform Lincoln that he was making it impossible for Kenney to do his job. The ghost did not appear to the bodyguard again. The wife of President Coolidge also met Lincoln once, while Eleanor Roosevelt and Dwight Eisenhower—who never actually saw the sixteenth president's spirit—both said that they felt the spirit's presence near them on several occasions.)

# 1940: The Ghost in the Garden

George O'Hara didn't believe the old stories.

George, the White House gardener, had heard that twenty years before, on instructions from First Lady Edith Wilson, gardeners had planned to make extensive changes in the Rose Garden. According to the stories, though, they were menaced by a ghost, and eventually Mrs. Wilson called off the project.

President Roosevelt enjoyed the Rose Garden, and as spring was approaching, O'Hara wanted to make his visits more scenic. With the approval of the First Lady, and disregarding warnings from veterans of the previous attempt to redesign the garden, the gardener set about his task.

Taking a stroll through the grounds prior to drawing up plans, O'Hara felt something sharp brush against his wrist. He looked down and saw scratches on his skin. He realized he must somehow have brushed against thorns.

Wiping the thin trail of blood with a handerchief, he sat down on the grass to sketch out a new design. And he heard a voice which seemed to whisper, "Mine."

O'Hara looked around. No one was there, and he ignored what must have been a ventilator or the wind.

After working all night on his plans, O'Hara and three assistants arrived early the next morning with four wheelbarrows of topsoil. The gardener had decided to add a horseshoe-shaped bed of roses around the garden, creating a new path around the perimeter, after which he would rearrange the layout of the garden proper.

As soon as the first shovel dug into the grass, the men heard a moan. They stopped and glanced at each other, then looked at O'Hara. He lit a cigarette and told them it must have been one of the wheelbarrows settling. He told them to return to their digging. Abruptly, one after the other, the wheelbarrows spilled over.

The men stopped again. Two of them threw down their shovels and left. The third, a veteran of the last group which had tried to redo the garden, looked at O'Hara.

"We aren't wanted here, Mr. O'Hara. Just like before."

O'Hara was staring at the wheelbarrows. "That's ridiculous. Go work on the hedges. I'll get this thing started and let you know when I need you."

The man tipped the brim of his cap and left.

When he was gone, O'Hara walked over to one of the wheelbarrows, set it upright, and kicked at it to try to make it fall over. It was steady as the U.S. government. Then he went to one of the shovels, picked it up, and used his foot to drive it hard into the ground.

*"Mine,"* a voice whispered, much louder than the last time.

O'Hara stopped. "Someone's pulling my leg," he complained, and storming over to a clump of nearby bushes, he pushed the shovel through them, looking to see if there was a hidden loudspeaker.

There was nothing in the bush. Stepping back, O'Hara flung his cigarette in the empty wheelbarrow and went back to the edge of the garden to resume the digging.

As soon as he put the shovel into the grass, something

grabbed it. He could neither push it in further nor withdraw it, and he stood back, staring at it. Suddenly, the shovel flew from the ground and beat him about the shins. When he tried to grab it, dirt showered up from the mounds of soil. Particles bit at his eyes and cheeks, and got in his mouth. After several seconds, both attacks ceased, and O'Hara ran over and picked up the shovel. He swung it around him, encountered nothing, and with a cry of exasperation threw it aside.

A security guard looked out at him just then, and O'Hara explained that he'd been stung by a bee. The guard seemed to accept that, and when he left, O'Hara spit out soil and lit another cigarette.

"Mine," he muttered under his breath. "First I hear things, now I see them."

The stories couldn't be true. There had to be a *logical* explanation for what was happening. Some new Pentagon weapon—a magnet gone haywire, causing crazy things to happen to the iron in the soil and in the shovel.

The damned shovel. He looked over at it, jumping to his feet when he saw a woman standing there. She was wearing a dress which belonged to another era, and neither the fabric nor her long hair was stirred by the wind.

"These gardens are mine," she said softly. "I planted them, and they are to remain as I planted them."

O'Hara said, "Miss, your *grandmother* wasn't alive when these gardens were planted. They were put in by Dolley Madison nearly two hundred years ago."

The woman was unfazed. She repeated that the garden was hers. O'Hara flicked his cigarette behind him, into the wheelbarrow. He intended to tell her that he worked for the president and had every intention of doing his job. But when he looked back again, the woman was gone.

Now he knew what the logical explanation was for all of this: he'd been working too hard and was imagining things, from flying dirt to attractive young women.

Shaking his head, he went to pick up the shovel. As he bent over it, the handle snapped in two, as though a great weight had been dropped on it. And as he looked down at the broken tool, he concluded that there *was* one other explanation.

Going over to the guard, O'Hara asked if he could use the White House library to look up some gardening information. There, the gardener went to a book about first ladies and looked up Dolley Madison. He stared at the picture, astonished. The likeness was exact.

The Rose Garden was not changed by George O'Hara or by anyone else. And it's said that the ghost of Dolley Madison still walks the grounds, protecting the home that was dear to her.

(Note: Dolley is also said to haunt the Octagon House in Washington, D.C., which is where she and her husband James resided after the White House was burned by the British during the War of 1812.)

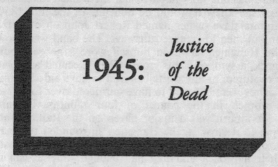

**1945:** *Justice of the Dead*

Doris Ackerman got more of an education than she bargained for.

Using the mid-semester break to work on her history thesis, the New York University graduate student drove to Woodburn, a stately old home in Dover, Delaware, which was once a stop on the old Underground Railroad—the route taken by slaves escaping from the south to the north. The mansion's owner, Quaker Daniel Cowgill, would provide the refugees with food and shelter during the day, and the former slaves would continue their flight under cover of darkness.

Doris reached the mansion late in the afternoon. She had written to the present owners, and though they had no ties to the brave Cowgill, they granted Doris permission to walk the grounds. She wanted to see what the escaped slaves had seen, look at the rooms in which they were sheltered, walk the hills they'd had to negotiate in the dead of night.

There was one story in particular she wanted to research, though she knew it would be difficult. In the mid-1850s, a Virginia slave owner named Robert Johnson organized a band of men to capture runaways. The band was known as the Hangmen; Johnson himself wore a noose around his neck, a symbol of his group. They executed any black they captured, or any white believed to have aided a runaway. They were believed to have murdered over forty men and women in the course of four months. Learning that Woodburn was a major haven on the Railroad and vowing to destroy it, the Hangmen surrounded the mansion one night. Fortunately, Cowgill had gotten wind of their approach and had had enough time to call on sympathizers from Dover to defend the estate. The Virginians were repulsed—save for Johnson, who refused to retreat or surrender. After the battle, Johnson was found hanging from a tree. The point Doris wanted very much to clear up was whether he had taken his own life, or whether Cowgill's people had executed him. She had a description of the tree, and knew the length of the rope Johnson wore. If she could find the tree, she would be able to determine whether Johnson could have knotted the short noose around a branch thick enough to hold him.

As the sun went down, Doris completed her tour of the inside of the mansion. Flashlight in hand, winter coat buttoned, she began walking among the pines and leafless poplars which ringed the estate.

Sitting on a bench several hundred yards from the mansion, Doris took out her notebook and, by the glow of the flashlight, began jotting down her impressions of the grounds at night. It was cold, like it had been on the February night of the assault, and she shivered as the chill wind swept over her. But that was good. She *wanted* to feel the way Johnson's and Cowgill's people had felt. Doris had been to enough historical sites to know that scenes of intense tragedy or triumph never quite surrendered the souls of the people who had lived or died there. And now, as she turned her back on the distant lights of the city and looked across the dark estate, she almost felt as though she was turning her back on the calendar. There *was* something here. Something trying to touch her.

Slipping the small reporter's notebook into her coat, Doris walked toward the position which Johnson was said to have held during the attack. The icy wind whipped at her cheeks, but she barely noticed. Being on part of the Railroad, she felt as she always did: that the ground was both hallowed and damned. She was humbled by the suffering the slaves had endured, yet proud that there were people like Cowgill who had helped to end their suffering.

Scattered snowflakes fell, glistening in the beam of her flashlight as she reached a small group of poplars. One of them was thick and bent, its branches twisted. This was the tree where Johnson was said to have been found. The limbs were spaced close enough together so that Johnson could have climbed to one high off the ground and taken his life. But it didn't make sense that he would have. The desperate radical would have rather spent his last moments on earth shooting people or, if he'd run out of ammunition, clubbing them with the butt of his rifle.

The old tree creaked in the wind. Twigs crackled underfoot as Doris walked behind the poplar and looked out at the mansion as Johnson would have seen it, trying to imagine herself in his position.

As she stood behind the tree, Doris felt something move and, moments later, heard a jangling above. She looked up, but saw nothing. Then she heard the limbs of the poplar groan beside her; not the creaking-door sounds they were making before, but a deep groaning, as though they were straining under some great weight.

Fearing a limb was about to break, she stepped back and passed the light up and down the length of the tree, then back again. She held it on a branch roughly ten feet from the ground.

A man's body was hanging from the limb and twisting gently in the wind. His arms had been pulled behind him and lashed with chains, and his lower legs had also been bound. He was dressed in a gray greatcoat and muddy riding boots; he wore a thin, black moustache and had thick, dark brows. From the one contemporary photograph she'd seen, Doris knew that the man was Robert Johnson.

She circled the tree, looking up, more excited than afraid. The man's hands and feet were chained: so he *had* been captured and killed. But by the Quaker Cowgill? That didn't correspond with what she knew of the man. And would he have let the refugees, guests at his home, murder the man? Wouldn't the good townspeople have wanted to put the killer on trial?

While she considered the different scenarios, Doris felt the others.

Her back was to the house and she didn't know who was there, but she knew that she and Johnson weren't alone. She continued around the tree, and when she was once again facing the estate, she shined her beam across the yard.

There were at least three dozen people standing before her. They were mostly slaves from their appearance, though several whites also stood in the crowd. Their expressions were grim and their bodies motionless, despite the cold and the snow. They didn't say anything, nor did they have to.

These were all the victims of Johnson and his men. And somehow, Doris understood their tacit message. When Cowgill had refused to allow the slaying of the slave owner, his victims had taken it upon themselves to perform the task. And they were still here, like the dead soldiers on a battlefield, an emotional presence which ensured that people would never forget what had happened here.

Doris looked across the solemn faces, branding the images in her brain, then turned off the light. As the beam died, so did the visions. Robert Johnson was also gone.

When she returned to her studies, Doris wrote evocatively of the battle at Woodburn and said of Robert Johnson that it would never be proven who had been responsible for his death. She did, however, theorize that he had fought until the end and was killed by slaves who were beyond Cowgill's control.

Just how *far* beyond Cowgill's control, she did not say.

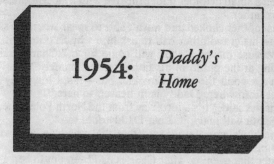

# 1954: *Daddy's Home*

Christmas at the Reynolds home in rural Maine wasn't the same without Dick.

The soldier had been killed by artillery at the Elbe River in April of 1945, as the U.S. Ninth Army marched toward Berlin. So destructive had the blasts been that it was weeks before they could identify Dick or his comrades. He left behind his pregnant young wife Janet and his grieving parents and brother.

The Reynoldses got together each year at the home of Dick's parents, where there was good food, shared affection, and tears. It became especially difficult for the family as the years went by and baby Charles looked and behaved more and more like his father. He smiled like Dick, had the same passion for pancakes, and even absently twirled a lock of hair when he was thinking as his father had done.

However, nothing affected them more than the Christmas eve when Charles did something he'd never done before:

placed a small cylinder under the tree with a label addressed to his father.

His mother choked and wasn't able to speak when she saw it, and his grandfather had to ask him why he'd done it.

"Because maybe Daddy will come for it," Charles said, looking at the photo of his father on the mantel.

"It's a good thought, Chuckie, but—it's a long way to travel from where Daddy is in heaven to here."

Charles said, "It's a long way from the North Pole to here, but Santa will make it. I bet Daddy does too."

The boy's grandfather said that that was true, and with tears in his eyes, he kissed the youngster's cheek.

Later that evening, after Charles had been put to bed and the family was sitting by the fire, the boy called for his mother. She went up to the guest room, unsettled by the thought that Charles's gift to his father had brought on a nightmare. The nightmares usually happened when she took him to little league games or went on a date—things he perceived as his father's responsibility.

The guest room was dark, and Janet felt her way around her bed to his—the bed in which Dick had slept as a boy. Charles was sitting up, his shoulders slumped forward but not trembling, as they usually were.

"What is it, hon?" she asked.

"Daddy was here." His voice was buoyant, and it scared her.

"Chuckie, you were dreaming."

"No," the boy insisted, "he was here. He wanted to thank me for leaving him a present. He thought it was funny that I put it inside toilet paper cardboard."

Janet sat on the bed and kissed Charles on the forehead. "It was a dream, honey. Now, go back to sleep, so Christmas will get here faster." She smiled conspiratorially. "And—this was supposed to be a secret—but when you get up, Grandma's going to make you a whole stack of pancakes with—"

"Ma, he's back!"

Janet's mouth snapped shut as she looked at her son. Charles was smiling, pointing behind her, waving.

"Charles, please stop."

"Lookit, Ma, he's holding up my drawing." The boy

frowned. "Hey, no fair! You promised not to open it till morning! Or is it morning already where you are?"

Janet looked at the luminous dial of the Hopalong Cassidy clock her mother-in-law had bought for Charles. Her heart thudded in her chest. It would already be Christmas in Germany.

"Charles, you know I don't like it when you tease."

"I'm *not* teasing! He's there! He's looking at you, now!"

Janet was still and cold, waves of goosebumps rising on her neck and arms. Part of her wanted to turn, to prove to her son that Dick wasn't there, but a larger part of her was afraid.

Still, she had to do it for her son, to show him that he was imagining things. She moved sideways on the bed, but kept her head straight down, staring into her lap. Then, taking a deep breath, she looked up quickly: the room was empty.

"I'm looking," she said sternly, "but I don't see anything except the walls."

"He's gone now," Charles said. "You took too long."

Janet fired him an angry look. "He *wasn't* there, and I'm very upset with you."

"But Ma!"

"'Ma' nothing. You go to bed, and we'll discuss this in the morning. And if I hear from you again, no pancakes."

Tucking the boy in, Janet went into the hallway and stood silently weeping outside the door for several minutes before going downstairs. Assuring everyone that Charles was all right, she sat down and stared vacantly at the brightly lit tree.

And noticed that Charles's gift to Dick was missing.

With a small cry, she leapt from her chair and ran up the stairs. She could hear Charles whispering. She ran into the room, flicked on the light, and looked at her son. He was sitting in his bed, smiling.

"Charles, *why* did you take the drawing back? Why are you doing this?"

"I didn't. Daddy did. And he promises he'll come and see me again."

"Your father isn't here!" she yelled, frightened and confused.

"But he was—"

"No! He wasn't! He *couldn't* have been!"

Charles began to cry, and Janet stared down at the boy's face, at Dick's face. At once, she was sorry she'd yelled; what harm was there in wishing *that* hard for something, wishing for something that she herself wanted so very badly.

"I'm sorry," she said, putting her arms around him. "If it makes you feel better to think that Daddy was here, I guess there's no harm—"

"I didn't *think* it, Mom. He was here."

"All right, he was here. But if he comes back, promise me something. Promise you'll tell him you have to get some sleep."

Charles hesitated. "What if Daddy says I can stay up?"

"He won't. He'll understand that you need your rest."

Charles didn't call down again, not that night or any other. And though he left gifts under the tree for the next few years, Dick never came for them. Janet was at once relieved and sad to know that Charles had imagined the visit.

When he was eighteen, Charles followed in his father's footsteps by enlisted in the military. He joined the air force, and was sent to South Vietnam in 1965 after Vietcong forces launched a ground attack against the American base at Pleiku. Shot down after a bombing run against the north, Charles miraculously made his way through one hundred miles of jungle, despite the fact that he was nearly blinded.

When he was found, emaciated and delirious, he said that he'd gotten out of the jungle by following his father. Upon learning of his safe return, Janet didn't care what her son believed, as long as he was alive.

Two weeks later, she received a parcel from the hospital. In it were dogtags and a note. Charles wrote, "I held on to these when I couldn't see. I told you he was there."

Janet looked at the dogtags, and then clutched them to her: they were not Charles's, but those of her husband, which had been lost when the artillery shell exploded.

She was, from that moment on, a most grateful believer.

# 1955: *Ghostly Warning*

It was early on a spring evening in Hawaii when the Schneider family came to believe in ghosts.

The Californians were camping just northwest of the Kau Desert, in the shadow of Mauna Loa's mighty Kilauea Crater. They were alone, most vacationers preferring the hotels and beaches to the wilds. Come morning, they planned to head to the volcano's lava fields, where they would do some hiking.

Burton Schneider was just starting a fire while his wife Cindy and fourteen-year-old daughter Myra gathered the food in their rented trailer. Teenage "Duke," having set up a small bridge table, was reading from a tour book.

"It says here that the most important of the Hawaiian gods is named Kane, and that he made the heaven and earth. You know, Dad—who's to say they're wrong and our god's the right one?"

"Nobody," Burton replied. "Maybe it's just two names for the same god."

"Or maybe *we're* wrong. Can you imagine that? Two zillion Christians and Jews and Hindus, all wrong. And a bunch of Hawaiians all—"

He was interrupted by shrieks from the trailer. The men looked over as Cindy and Myra rushed out.

"Did you see that?" Cindy yelled.

"See what?"

"The whole trailer was shaking! Did we have an earthquake?"

"I didn't feel anything," Duke said. "You sure Myra wasn't playing one of her Four Coins records too loud?"

Myra made a face, and her mother frowned. "You mean you two didn't see a thing?"

Burton shook his head, but said he'd check the tires as soon as he got the fire going.

Five minutes later, he walked toward the front of the camper. In the fading light, it didn't look as if any of the tires on the right side had lost air. He went around the front of the vehicle to check the left side. That was when he saw the grille and stopped.

"Oh, great. How did *this* happen?"

Duke ran over, the women followed, and they stood staring at the grille. It had been dented in several places.

"Maybe whatever shook the trailer did that," Myra said.

"Yeah, right," said Duke. "Giant ants, like in *Them.*"

Myra looked around nervously.

"You must've kicked up some rocks," Cindy said.

"In front?" Burton shook his head. "Even if we had, they wouldn't have done this kind of damage."

Just then, there was a muted pop where the trailer overhung the cab, and glass rained down from the front window. Moments later, the cap popped off the water tank on the side of the vehicle, and the contents gushed out.

"Did we rent a lemon or what?" Duke asked, as Burton ran over to close off the water. But the cap had been crushed into an oval shape and couldn't be replaced, and he stood there, helpless, as the contents drained into the sand.

"So much for camping out," Myra said, with some relief.

"Nuts to that!" Duke said. "We've got jars of juice. We just can't flush the toilet."

Burton said, "That doesn't explain why any of this happened."

"Maybe Kane isn't happy we're here," Duke offered.

"Who's Kane?" Myra asked, and while Duke explained, Burton wondered if a day in the sun hadn't somehow caused the metal to expand and a few seams to pop. Regardless, his son was right: they could live two days without the toilet.

The hamburgers they cooked were delicious, and the night air was warm and delightful as the Schneiders sat at the table playing rummy. They didn't forget what had happened, but they tried to ignore it. Someone at Burton's engineering firm once told him that even the laws of physics were sometimes broken, and maybe this was just one of those times.

Suddenly, the trailer began to shake again. This time, however, it didn't stop after a few seconds. The trailer continued to rock back and forth, even as Burton approached. He went into the cab, checked the emergency brake and gear shift, then stood outside and scratched his head. He looked toward the crater. There was smoke rising from it—"safe smoke," they called it, since it rarely betokened a serious eruption. Maybe Cindy had been right. Maybe this was some kind of very local earthquake.

Climbing back into the cab, he started up the engine. As soon as he did so, it stopped shaking. He moved the trailer several hundred yards to the other side of the fire.

"That should do it," he said, and turned to go back to the table. However, he hadn't taken more than two steps when the fire went out. It didn't die, it was killed; snuffed, as though it had been sucked into the ground. The silence deepened and the darkness seemed heightened by the brilliant stars and faint glow from the crater.

Cindy called her husband's name, but before Burton could answer, Myra began to scream.

"No—*no!*"

Sitting next to her, Duke reached out in the darkness and touched her shoulders: she was shaking wildly.

"Sis, what is it?"

"The fire . . . so *hot!*"

"What fire? The fire blew out."

"The volcano! Don't! *Don't!*"

The girl began chattering wildly in a language none of them recognized, and in a voice that hardly seemed like hers. Cindy sobbed with fear as Burton felt his way over. He took out his lighter, flicked it on, and recoiled: the young woman at the table hardly seemed like his daughter. She was shaking violently and her eyes were wide, her expression contorted with terror. Her flesh was ruddy and perspiration ran down her cheeks and forehead.

"Pele!" she screamed. "Pele!"

"What's *wrong* with her?" Cindy screamed.

*"Pele!"* she repeated again and again, slapping at her sides and arms, screaming toward the heavens, snapping her head violently from side to side.

"Pele?" Duke said. "Hey, I know that name. It's in the tour book."

"Duke, not *now!*"

Burton used his handkerchief to wipe Myra's face. Her hands were clenched, and she was pulling in her legs, as though trying to lift them off the ground. Cindy wept as she held the lighter for Burton and watched helplessly.

"Dad, don't you see?"

"See *what?*"

"There's some kind of *spirit* in her."

"Duke—"

"No, it makes sense: a sacrifice victim to Pele, the goddess who causes the lava to flow. What happened to the trailer, and now this—she's doing everything she can to warn us away."

"You're out of your mind!"

"You think so? Put her in the trailer and let's go. I guarantee you, Myra will come back."

Near tears, Cindy urged Burton to try it, to try anything before their daughter had a stroke.

Reasoning that they'd have to get her to a doctor anyway, Burton put his arms around his daughter's waist and told Cindy to take her legs. While his parents put Myra into bed, Duke folded away the table and started the engine.

As soon as they were away from the volcano, heading

north to Hilo, the girl stopped shaking. In less than an hour, she was sitting up, sipping juice, talking with her mother. She had no recollection of what had happened to her.

The following day, the crater erupted, spewing boiling mud where the Schneiders would have been hiking. And the next time they worshipped, they took a moment to thank Kane—and the nameless girl who had saved their lives.

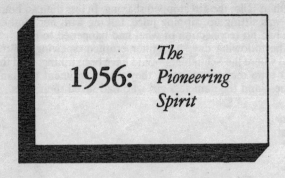

# 1956:    *The Pioneering Spirit*

It was not the kind of story Will had become a journalist to write.

A free-lance writer, forty-year-old Will Bever covered politics for national magazines and a major wire service. His style was cynical and his readership loyal, but the election was over and things were quiet in Washington. When one of his editors called and offered to send him west, all expenses paid, Will accepted. It was not just because the story piqued his interest, but because he had written so long about outlaws in Washington that he figured it was time to turn his attention to outlaws of the Old West.

On December 11, he packed his bags and flew to Albuquerque, New Mexico. There, Will was to research the infamous Ben Reed, who, just before the turn of the century, had made his living by sheltering escaped bandits, killers, and other criminals.

Leasing a car, Will drove one hundred miles then eventually left his car and rented a pair of horses from a rancher a dozen miles from the area known as Reed Canyon. He stayed the night at the ranch and set out the next morning. Over breakfast, the reporter asked the rancher what he knew about Reed.

"Nobody knows much about him," he said. "Old Man Reed died a half-century ago plus six. Had a shack, pretty rundown; it's still there, I reckon. No one's been up there that I know."

"I'm surprised. Haven't people looked for the money he took from outlaws?"

"No," the rancher replied. "Not recently, anyway."

The old rancher wasn't sure where Reed's house was, except that it was somewhere toward the top of the canyon.

The rancher was impressed as the neat easterner strapped his tent and provisions to one of the two large Appaloosas he'd rented him.

"Ya seem to know what yer doin', horsewise."

"I grew up on a farm in Maryland," he said.

The rancher dug the toe of his boot in the ground.

"Mind if I ask you if you know what yer doin'—ghostwise?"

Will stopped and stared at him. "Are you going to tell me that Ben Reed is up there, haunting his homestead?"

The rancher shook his head. "No, sir. I'm not going to tell you anything like that. I *am* going to tell you that years ago, people used to see folks up there, folks dressed funny. Lookin' funny. Men, women, an' kids. No one goes up there anymore. But sometimes, on the night wind, ya can hear things that ain't coyotes."

Thanking the man for the warning, Will mounted up. If nothing else, the ghost angle would add some color to the story.

According to the research Will had done, this region had once been part of a trail used by settlers heading west during the latter half of the nineteenth century. Clearly, it hadn't changed much in one hundred years. The dirt trail was still there, plants grew wild, and rockslides lay where they had fallen. The only thing that surprised Will was that the nearer he got to his goal, the sparser the fauna became. Rabbits, foxes, even birds grew scarce, and only insects remained plentiful. His horses were clearly uneasy, too, snorting and hesitating and finally protesting so strongly that he decided to make camp and explore on foot.

According to the one article he'd read mentioning Reed, the trail was visible from the shack. There were two cliffs overlooking the dirt road. Will decided to climb the north one first.

By nightfall, he'd found nothing. "Which figures," he wrote when he returned to his tent, just before nightfall. "I always back losers in elections as well. I may just change my name to Dewey Stevenson."

Letting the campfire burn itself out, Will climbed into his sleeping bag shortly after eleven. Exhausted from the climb, he fell asleep quickly. Even the restless sounds made by the horses failed to keep him awake.

Not so the clatter which echoed along the canyon walls. The din drew him from sleep. At first he thought it was the horses stomping on rocks or gear, but then he realized the horses were on the other side of the tent, on the western side.

He lay there and listened, assuming it was a cart or car entering the canyon.

The temperature had plummeted, the fire had died, and a gentle but chill wind crept under the tent walls. Will didn't want to leave his bag. But the sound grew more expansive, obviously stretching across a good length of the trail, and, pulling a flashlight from his duffel bag, he wormed forward and poked his head from the tent.

What he saw wasn't real. It couldn't be.

Coming over a rise was a line of people, horses, dogs, and covered wagons. They were ragged, dressed in clothing from about a century ago, and moving slowly. A few of the men wore the remnants of what looked like Union uniforms.

But their dress aside, these weren't like any people or things he had ever seen, even at all-night Washington parties. Everyone and everything in the procession was the same pale, white color, but the consistency seemed to change, like water moving under thick ice.

Now he could actually see through part of one, now he couldn't.

The beam of the flashlight passed through the things it touched, though it caused their viscous insides to glow.

He shut off the light, convinced it was a trick of the beam. But with a faint, hazy glow, the wagon train continued to move past him. The cold wind he noticed seemed to come from them: it didn't blow, but radiated from the figures less than fifty yards away.

Will reached around and grabbed his camera. The clicking drew no attention. He exposed an entire roll.

More curious than frightened, Will put the camera aside, pulled on his jacket, and walked over.

None of the people spoke. None looked over. He reached out to touch one, a man walking alongside a wagon and carrying a rifle, but his hand passed through the man's shoulder. Will withdrew it quickly, the intense cold stinging his flesh.

He took several steps back. His own horses were bucking wildly now. He went over to try to calm them, but had little success.

Fearful that he would lose them, Will finally took his notebook, camera, and canteen, and rode off.

It was three A.M., and he spent the rest of the night riding around outside Reed Canyon. He waited until well after dawn before going back.

The horses were skittish, but nothing like the night before. He tied them up beside his tent and went to examine the trail. There were no marks, nothing to indicate that anyone had passed. He followed the road for nearly a mile on foot, and saw no trace of the specters who had passed that way.

Will returned to Washington, but the story he wrote never ran. The pictures showed nothing, not even smudges of white on black; he even doubted himself what he'd seen.

Years later, while researching another article, he learned that in 1866 a band of pioneers, including many Civil War veterans, set out for California. Most never arrived, and the graves of many members were found over a year later by another group of settlers.

Several settlers swore, though, that during their trek, they saw "shapes" that were not of this world.

Though Will took the phenomenon in stride, his work to keep politicians honest became even more relentless. Given the bittersweet, eternal quest of the pioneers he'd seen, it was, he felt, the very least he could do.

# 1957:  Riding the Rails

Jimmy Cubb had had it.

The ten-year-old North Carolinian had brought home a bad report card and, as a result, was forbidden to watch TV or read comic books until his grades improved.

No more Superman. No more Hopalong Cassidy. No more fun.

And no more mom and dad.

After his father laid down the law, Jimmy decided to run away from Maco, his hometown. Waiting until they were asleep, he grabbed a few of his favorite comics, a change of underwear and socks, a book of matches, and a box of Corn Flakes, stuffed them in his bookbag, and set out into the night. He left his notebook in the satchel. If he got cold, he'd burn it.

Jimmy had a destination in mind. He'd seen commercials on TV for careers in shipping. He'd leave Maco and head east to see if he could work on one of the boats that went from the Corncake Inlet out to the ocean. He would sail away like one of the men in the stories he half-heard in class, and come back home grown and rich, with ships of his own.

Nearly an hour after he set out through the hills behind his father's out-of-the-way auto-repair shop, the dark countryside was swept with a warm wind. Soon it was carrying a misty rain, then a storm. Thinking he'd better sit it out, Jimmy reluctantly ran to the bridge which crossed a nearby stream.

He took shelter there only reluctantly, because the bridge was near the railroad tracks of the Seaboard Coast Line.

Jimmy slogged down a muddy hill, slipping and skidding halfway down on his side, ending up in the stream which ran under the bridge, and finally crawling under the old, dark bridge.

He opened his bookbag and poured out the water. Pieces of the disintegrated Corn Flakes box flopped out. He sat there, shivering, trying not to think about the tracks just a short walk away.

The tracks—and the ghost light.

He tried to look on the good side. At least he wasn't as scared as he was when his Uncle Fred first told him the story.

It happened in the late 1860s, his uncle had said. Conductor Joe Baldwin was a man in the grand tradition of the great railroad conductors: a lifelong trainman, a man dedicated to serving the passengers and the big, beautiful engines and cars of the trains which carried them.

Walking along the tracks after the worst of a severe rainstorm had passed, Joe was making sure no mudslides or fallen limbs were blocking the tracks. It was still raining, and he held his light before him, squinting into the lingering storm.

Unfortunately, Joe Baldwin slipped on a wet tie and struck his head hard against the track. Dazed, he was unable to move when the train came by.

Jimmy could still see his uncle skid one hand across the other hard, could still hear the slap, as he said, "And just like *that*, Jimmy, the churning metal wheels rolled over poor Joe's neck, and his head went tumbling away like a cabbage."

Uncle Fred didn't know whether the stray head had rolled along the tracks or into the stream or somewhere else. He said for all he knew, "someone may have picked it up and used it as a doorstop." Obviously, Joe Baldwin didn't know where his head had gone either, for it was said that he often scoured the area on rainy nights, his lantern held high, still looking for his head.

"But it's just a story," Jimmy told himself now as he sat hugging his knees to his chest with one arm, bracing himself on the slope with the other. He was listening to the rain, his eyes shut, and imagining that it wasn't a storm but the wonderful sound of his mother sizzling bacon. They probably didn't cook bacon on ships, he told himself.

For a moment, the insides of his eyelids went red. Then comforting blackness returned.

"It was the headlights of a car," he told himself, shivering now from more than the dampness. But he didn't hear the engine or the whoosh of the tires on the road, and began to wonder.

Still, he didn't open his eyes.

Then the red flash came again. Brighter. And he thought —but wasn't sure—that he heard the *squoosh* of feet in the muck.

"Daddy?"

Maybe he hadn't been as quiet as he'd thought. Maybe his father had followed him.

*"Dad?"*

But if he had, why wasn't he answering?

The dripping of water from the bridge had washed away some of the soil beside him. His hand was resting on something hard. A rock?

Or a skull?

*Was it Joe Baldwin's head?*

Screaming, Jimmy opened his eyes and, leaving his bookbag behind, began running up the slope to the hills. A light illuminated the ground in front of him. He didn't look back to see why. He lost his footing, was on all fours, but scrambled up the hill like a marine. When he reached the top, the light came on again and threw his shadow in front of him.

Jimmy didn't even try to be silent when he reached the house.

He exploded through the back door, screaming for his parents, promising to get good grades, and promising even more fervently that he was home to stay.

Half asleep, his parents wrapped him in a bath towel, gave him warm milk, and listened to his story. There was no punishment. The terror in Jimmy's eyes showed that he had received punishment enough.

The following morning, Jimmy and his father walked over to the bridge.

There were footprints in the mud, and the contents of Jimmy's satchel had been strewn over the area.

"It must have been a hobo," Jimmy's father said.

Jimmy nodded. But as they were leaving, he noticed something that gave him nightmares for months:

There was a big hole beside where he'd been sitting.

A hole where his hand had been.

A hole just about the size of a head.

# 1958: A Portrait of Hannah

The stories didn't bother Robert Kidder, not one bit. In fact, the artist rather enjoyed owning a piece of local history, quirky though it was.

When Kidder gave up the advertising rat race in New York and moved to Newfield, Maine, to paint, he bought a house that had been built 160 years before. However, it wasn't just age which made the house interesting. The original owner, the redoubtable Hannah Chadbourne—a distant relative, it was said, of Miles Standish—so loved the home she and her late husband had built, that when she lay on her deathbed in 1826, she made her son and brother promise that she would never have to leave it.

The men vowed that she never would. They said that they would bury her in the backyard, beside the pine tree she herself had planted.

The frail old woman seemed horror-struck. She reached up, grabbed her son's arm, and shook her head violently.

"No!" she wheezed. "I do not want to be outside the house. I must be buried *inside.*"

She insisted on being buried beneath the kitchen, where the wood was forever scented with the aroma of her famed cherry pies.

So insistent was she that the men acceded to her wishes. When she died that night, they tore up the floorboards somewhere in the kitchen and buried Hannah beneath the house.

At first, people shunned the place, feeling that what had been done was sinful. But over the years they took a less censorious view. The interred became something of a local gremlin, folks blaming "Hard-Headed Hannah" whenever milk was spilled or a cake failed to rise or some other misfortune struck someone's kitchen.

Occupants of the house tended to take a more charitable view of old Hannah, since even the least superstitious of them didn't want to say or do anything that might offend their "guest."

Kidder wasn't like that.

Fascinated by the tales, he decided to make the old woman the subject of his first painting. If nothing else, he was sure he could get the town hall to display it, maybe even make a sale.

Excited and anxious to begin, he started the very night he moved in.

Since no paintings of Hannah existed, Kidder first made several studies in charcoal. Taking his portable easel into the kitchen for inspiration, he sat at the table, trying to imagine what she would have been like puttering around the small rooms with their low, beamed ceilings.

Five cups of coffee later, he had come up with a long face, sunken eyes, a severe mouth, and a wispy cloud of white hair.

He sketched it roughly from several angles, then went to make a fresh pot of coffee before playing any more with the drawings.

As he stood at the sink, filling the percolator, he heard a clacking sound in the wide pantry to his left.

His first thought was that it was the hot water coursing

through the pipes, causing them to clatter. His second thought was that it was mice. This was, after all, a house with some years on it.

Setting the coffee-maker aside, he opened the old door and jumped back as his broom and dustpan tumbled out.

Picking up the broom and dustpan, he leaned them back so they wouldn't go sliding again. Glancing down, he noticed that the wood of the floor here was slightly different from that in the rest of the kitchen. He felt a chill as he realized that this was where Hannah must have been buried.

He snickered as the ghoulish thought occurred to him that if he dug her up, he'd be able to get a look at her facial structure. And would probably have nightmares for the rest of his life, and *then* some.

When his coffee was ready, Kidder returned to the small easel.

His charcoal was missing. He looked around, felt in his pockets, looked in the pantry and even in the coffee tin. He had no idea where he'd left it, and went to the bedroom to get another piece from his kit.

There was a short woman standing before it. She was dressed in a housecoat with frill on the hem and on the sleeves. Her long hair was gray, shot through with red.

And the face! It was round, with a heavy brow, a broad mouth, and a tiny chin. The big eyes were far apart.

The woman shuffled toward him, preceded by the reek of damp earth. Kidder was too startled to move. He watched as the woman stretched out a pale hand, opened it, and held the missing piece of charcoal toward him.

He still didn't budge. And suddenly, like Marley's ghost, the woman vanished. The charcoal dropped to the floor. He left it and hurried out.

Confused and a little frightened, Kidder concluded that either he couldn't keep the hours he did when he was an art student, or he was losing his mind.

He didn't like the third option he considered: that Hannah was up and about and keeping an eye on him.

Returning to the kitchen, he poured another cup of coffee, then sat heavily at the table. He gazed down at the face on his sketch pad.

The faces he'd drawn were all crossed out. At the edge of the page was another; a portrait, almost like a child's drawing, showing a round face, with a thick brow and a wide mouth carefully balanced on a nub of a chin. The eyes were large and far apart.

Just like the face in the bedroom.

Kidder's fear suddenly left him. He didn't particularly relish the idea of having a ghost as an art critic. But it was in a strange way comforting to know that he had an audience. An *interested* audience.

He executed the painting during the next several days.

Over the years, Kidder sold landscapes and still lifes and did portraits of local kids and couples and dogs. But he never sold the portrait of Hannah. Few who came to the house even knew he'd painted it, for it remained, ornately framed, in the dark of the pantry, where he knew it would be appreciated.

For the youth of America, the shock of his death was unparalleled: George Reeves, the all-American actor who'd co-starred in *Gone with the Wind, Samson and Delilah,* and *From Here to Eternity,* and had most notably played Superman on TV for five glorious years, was dead of a gunshot wound.

When it happened in June of 1959, kids had a difficult time digesting the fact that, allegedly, the actor had been despondent over being typecast—whatever that meant—and had put a gun to his head in the middle of the night.

Friends who were staying in the house that evening all said they heard only one shot. However, police found *three* holes; one in Reeves and two in the wall. All came from a non-repeating Luger.

People who loved and worked with Reeves believed he was murdered and that there was a coverup. For months, he had been pursued by the wife of a powerful Hollywood movie mogul. When she refused to give the actor up, her husband, it is believed, made the decision for her.

For a time, Reeves's home on a quiet stretch of Benedict Canyon Road became a shrine of sorts, visited by the curious and by sensation-seekers. During a subsequent, short-lived investigation demanded by Reeves's mother, who died not long after it was begun, police were assigned to watch the place.

Nor were they alone.

After dinner one night, ten-year-old Jimmy Stein biked down to the house from his own home near Beverly Glen Park, a long ride of four miles. He was a big fan of Superman, the Lone Ranger, and the other television heroes. Just over a year after the fact, he was still upset about the death of one of his idols. He had once gone to Reeves's house when he was alive and waited in vain for him to come home to get his autograph. He needed to go there again, to find a keepsake, a memento. It was wrong, he knew, and his conscience troubled him about it. But he wanted to have part of George Reeves with him, always, and he didn't think the actor would mind. Superman liked kids.

The house looked the same. Set back slightly from the road, shaded by trees. Watched by a pair of police officers.

They were sitting in their patrol car, parked on the street. He got off his bike two houses away, laid it on the curb, and snuck quietly through the trees to the house. In the twilight, he approached unseen.

Stopping behind a garbage pail, he listened to the officers chatting. He got their names: Charles and T.H. Incredibly, they weren't talking about George Reeves. They were talking about a sports car.

He didn't understand how they could be sitting there doing that when they had the honor of watching over the home of the great Mr. Reeves. They should have been talking about him and his show. Not that adults ever did what made sense.

As Jimmy settled down and began thinking about how he might get inside, he saw both officers look toward the house.

A light had gone on downstairs.

"I thought the place was empty," T.H. said.

"Like a turkey pen the day after Thanksgiving," Charles replied. "I checked myself."

"Back windows all locked?"

"Every one."

They got out of the car and stood by the passenger's side. The light went off. A moment later, another flicked on upstairs.

"Probably some goddamn souvenir hunter," T.H. grumbled. "Let's go chase them out."

Jimmy felt his throat constrict. Maybe it wouldn't be so easy to get inside unseen. On the other hand, who'd be dumb enough to break into a house and turn on lights?

Suddenly three shots popped inside the house. They were followed by a woman's scream. Drawing their guns, the two officers ran ahead, going through the unbolted front door.

Jimmy snuck along after them, ducking in when they ran upstairs. He hid behind a sofa.

A few minutes later, the officers came downstairs. Charles was shaking his head.

"It had to be from somewhere else."

"Echoes, huh?"

"Sure," Charles said. "Car backfiring, someone startled by it."

"And the lights?"

"Loose bulb. Crazy circuit. Who the hell knows?" He looked at his partner. "What, you think the place is haunted?"

T.H. frowned. "Sure. And my name's Cosmo Topper."

The men left, closing the door behind Jimmy. The house suddenly seemed very *much* haunted. Pipes groaned and wood popped and the outside world seemed very far away.

Cautiously, the boy ventured from his hiding place. The sound of his own footsteps seemed magnified, like he weighed a ton. He walked toward the stairs on tiptoe, taking big, arcing steps, as though that would lessen the sound.

"Going somewhere, young man?"

Jimmy stopped dead in mid-stride. The voice wasn't that of either police officer; it was smoother. Stronger.

Familiar.

Now it was his bowels and not just his throat which tightened. He tasted his dinner in the back of his throat.

"Don't you know you're trespassing?"

The boy would have answered if he could, but he could barely breathe. He rolled his eyes around, but couldn't see far enough behind him. He'd have to move his whole head to see who was there—as if he didn't know. Though his neck didn't want to cooperate, somehow he forced his head to turn. When he saw who was there, his eyes went very, very wide.

Standing by the sofa was George Reeves, his hands on his hips, chin up, chest expanded. He was wearing his Superman costume, which was a muddy brown color. His skin was white. There was a raw hole in the side of his head.

"Well?"

"I'm s-s-sor-ry," Jimmy said, in a cracked whisper.

A smile played around the lips of the dead man. "What did you come for?"

"A s-souvenir, Mr. Super—, Mr. Reeves. Sir. But I . . . was wrong to. I'll go."

The figure faded quickly, but Jimmy stood for a long while, not moving. When he finally found his legs again, he ran to the back of the house, opening a window to let himself out.

Jimmy had his souvenir: a memory that would be as vivid when he was forty as it was when he was ten.

(Note: Over twenty years later, a TV crew shooting a special in the house also saw Reeves's ghost. Unfortunately, they were not quick enough to capture the apparition on film.)

**1961:** *Flier by Night*

Bobby lived in the pleasant New York suburb of Green Acres, on Long Island. The eight-year-old was an only child. His father sold insurance, and his mother taught piano.

Bobby enjoyed school more than he did summer vacations. Summers were lonely times because most of the neighborhood children went to camp. Since both of his parents worked, the family never got to go on trips. The boy spent most of his time reading comics or playing with his cowboy and Indian figures in a nearby lot where there was nothing but dirt, rubbish, and a dilapidated, green shack. Here and there, poking through the dirt, were patches of concrete, the remnants of an old airfield.

The nights were time for playing of a different kind.

Lying in bed, the window open, he would hear the planes as they flew over from nearby Idlewild Airport. When he was unable to sleep, he would pretend that he was a knight and they were roaring dragons. When he was drowsy, they always sounded like faraway thunder.

Then, one night, they sounded like a deep voice calling to him.

When he heard it, Bobby opened his eyes. He saw nothing but the pale moonlight throwing a faint glow across the plastic models he and his father had built.

The voice came again.

*"Bobbbyyyy."*

He squinted into the dark and saw a man standing by the door. Bobby screamed as soon as he saw the man; the man vanished even before Bobby's mother arrived.

Bobby didn't even pretend to be brave. He told her he'd had a nightmare and asked if he could sleep with his parents. His mother nodded, and Bobby followed her into the bedroom. She grumbled that this was the last time she'd let him read comic books before bed.

Bobby spent the next day playing in the lot and taking a bike ride to the store for more comics. By nighttime, the vision was barely half-remembered. He fell asleep quickly.

The man came to Bobby again in the bellowing of a jet.

*"Bobbbbyy."*

His eyes snapped open. His small heart thumped hard as he lay still and scouted the darkness, wide-eyed.

Something moved by the bureau where most of the models sat; the man stepped toward him, but Bobby didn't scream. He couldn't. Fear clogged his throat.

The man bowed stiffly, walked slowly into the moonlight in the center of the room, then stopped.

He was dressed in a brownish uniform, and was wearing a scarf, goggles, and a tight, leather cap. The glass of the goggles was broken; his black gloves were tattered. There were dark streaks on his face.

*"Bobbbyy. Come."*

Despite his ragged appearance, there was something soothing about his voice. Bobby hesitated, remembering what his mother had said about going anywhere with strangers. But this man wasn't a stranger, somehow. His voice was as familiar as the roar of the airplanes. Bobby swung from beneath the thin sheet and walked up to the man.

The man looked down at him, the moon glinting in each shard of the broken glasses.

*"Walk . . . with . . . me,"* he said softly, and held out his hand.

Bobby pulled on his Keds and took the man's hand. The glove felt warm and damp.

"Where are we going?"

The man didn't answer, and they walked out the door together.

The lights were off in his parents' room, and Bobby grew afraid again as they walked out the front door. He didn't remember opening it, but he must have; they were on the sidewalk.

The pair walked along Forest Road, to the lot. The man stopped at the far end of the shack. He pointed to the ground and asked Bobby to dig.

"Here?" He pointed down.

The man nodded and, kneeling in his pajama-shorts, Bobby picked up a broken slat and began jabbing at the ground.

Just below the surface, he found a wallet and a crucifix. He picked them up.

"Are these yours?" he asked, looking up.

The man was gone.

"Mister?"

Bobby rose, turned around.

"Mister, where did you go?"

He walked around the shack, and when he couldn't find him he grew scared again. Running all the way home, Bobby slowed as he approached the door, entered quietly, then dove into his bed and under the sheet.

The next thing he felt was his mother kissing his cheek. Bobby opened his eyes; the room was filled with sunlight. He looked at his mother, and felt the wallet and cross in his hand, beneath the cover.

"Mom," he said warily, "I . . . I have something to show you."

Sitting up, he produced the two objects and watched his mother's face darken.

"Where did you get these?"

He didn't tell her about the man. She'd only say he imagined it and then would take away his comics. He said simply, "I found them in the lot. Last night."

"Last *night?*"

Bobby's mother called to her husband, who was more interested in the objects than in his son's midnight journey. The ID in the wallet was dated 1934, and belonged to an Elliot Carter of Freeport.

Leaving his flustered wife behind, he went to the telephone directory and looked up the name. There were several Carters, though no Elliot; he phoned each in turn, asking to speak with Elliot.

The third call, to a woman, drew an angry response.

"Is this a joke of some kind? My husband died nearly thirty years ago."

"No, Mrs. Carter," he said. "I have his wallet here. And a cross."

There was a long, thick silence. The woman said she'd come that night to examine them.

Mrs. Celia Carter arrived after dinner. She was a hard-looking woman in her early fifties; she seemed more suspicious than grateful as she was shown in.

Bobby's father got the wallet and cross from the top of the dining-room hutch. The woman gasped when she saw them.

"They're his," she said, sitting down. "Where did you find them?"

"I didn't," the man said. "My son did. Where the airfield used to be."

The woman said nothing for several moments. Then she wiped a tear from her eye and said softly, "Elliot tested airplanes for the government. He died in a crash in 1934. He probably left these because he had a feeling. He always trusted his feelings."

She took a calming breath and opened the wallet. Inside was a photograph of her with her husband. She wept when she saw it; Bobby looked over her shoulder.

It was a picture of a woman standing beside a man in a flying suit, The same man who had come to visit him.

The woman rewarded Bobby with a five-dollar bill, and left with the mementoes. The man never came to Bobby again, but each night, as he listened to the airplanes passing overhead, they were never again dragons or thunder, but the voice of a man he would never forget.

**1963:** *The Approach of Winter*

Father Hammond was having difficulty sleeping.

It was nothing new; the sixty-six-year-old priest had been having trouble for over three years, since he had come to Boston from a small church in the country.

There was nothing he could put his finger on, other than a sense that the delicate balance between good and evil was more delicate than ever. The threat of nuclear war. Negroes being beaten in the streets with impunity, before the eyes of television cameras. People turning from faith more and more to material things. Shocking examples of what the bishop himself had called "a grave new world."

As he did most nights, the clergyman read from the New Testament. He preferred John for its beautiful language, above all. Then he walked about the fenced-in grounds. He was searching for hope in faith, and in the youth of the country, from its president to its bright students to its doctors, even to its inspiring astronauts.

There was more noise in the city than there used to be, too, even at eleven and twelve o'clock. More televisions heard through open windows. Louder music. A societal pressure cooker leaking around the edges.

During this late fall night, with a winter chill in the air, Father Hammond was walking behind the fence near midnight when he heard a clattering in the church.

*A rat,* he thought, and stopped. Hands clasped behind his back, head cocked, he listened. For a long moment there was nothing, and then he heard what sounded like sobs.

There was no one else here, or at least there shouldn't have been. The gate was locked, and the custodian had finished his work over an hour before.

Turning back down the slate path, the cool wind carrying a salty smell from the harbor, Father Hammond approached the dark church. There was a faint glow coming through the stained glass above the lintel—which surprised him, since it had been dark before.

Entering, the priest saw that the altar candlestick had been lit. He stood still, afraid until his faith took over. Uttering a prayer, he walked forward, heard the gentle sobbing again, and turned toward the confessional. The sound was coming from there.

"Hello?"

The priest's call went unanswered, though the sobbing continued.

Seating himself on the other side of the booth, Father Hammond prepared to hear confession. As he did so, the sobbing stopped, the candle went out, and the church was once again silent.

Father Hammond sat, listening for a moment, then stepped from the confessional. The church was empty. He walked to all the doors. Save for the door in the north transept, leading to the courtyard, all were locked.

Confused, the clergyman retired to the rectory and went to bed.

He was awakened in the middle of the night by more sounds of sobbing. Pulling on a robe, Father Hammond hurried to the church. The candle was once again lit and he entered quietly, so as not to disturb his mysterious visitor.

A man was kneeling by the high altar. He wore a suit, the back of which seemed to glisten in the faint light of the candle. He was sobbing, his face in his hand.

The priest approached slowly. When he was only a few paces away, he said, "My son, is there some way I can help you?"

The candle went out and the figure vanished, blending in with the shadows. Startled, Father Hammond stood there staring at the spot, wondering whether he had witnessed a miracle, or something more ominous.

The priest remained by the altar that night, praying.

The following day, John Kennedy was assassinated in Dallas. The president had worshipped here several times, and Father Hammond had heard his confession here once. The shock was overwhelming.

That night, after ministering to the emotional wounds of so many of his shocked parishioners, Father Hammond remained in the nave, praying for the nation.

Near midnight, the figure reappeared.

The candle ignited by itself, and the figure knelt, sobbing once more, by the altar.

Only this time, there was a difference: there was blood on its back. Stifling a gasp, the priest suddenly realized what it was.

The manifestation—ghost or angel, or even something dark from inside his own soul—had assumed the likeness of the slain president. The previous night it had foreshadowed today's sorrow; this night, it was succumbing to it.

Though the priest wished to speak, to say something consoling, he left the presence alone. He fell to his knees and prayed, unafraid. For he knew that while this was a minion of death, they were both praying for the same thing: the future of the nation, and for hope, which had that day been so savagely destroyed.

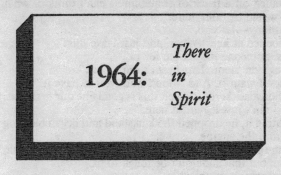

# 1964: *There in Spirit*

Newlyweds Anthony and Maria Borelli were driving cross-country for their honeymoon. They'd started out in the snow-covered New York suburb of Mamaroneck, bound for Los Angeles. Three days later, in the Ford Falcon he'd customized in his father's repair shop, they were on a bare stretch of Interstate 10 in warm and sunny Arizona. They had just passed through Bowie and planned to stop in Willcox for lunch.

Anthony slowed when he saw the dark mound shimmering against the pale, yellow expanse of desert.

"You see that? It looked like a bike."

Pulling over, Anthony got out and ran down the long embankment. Maria joined him.

At the bottom, lying on its side, was a motorcycle.

"This is wild," Anthony said. "Lookit. A vintage machine —twenty years old, at least. And no driver, no skidmarks, no nothin'." He squatted to examine it. "A few dents. It had to've fallen off a truck or somethin'. I can't think of what else it would be doin' here."

"Anthony—let's go."

He looked at her. "What, and just leave this?"

"Yes. Someone may come for it."

"Tough on them. This beaut's ours, now."

"I don't want it. And I don't want you to have it."

Anthony snickered. "Then this is gonna be our first spat, 'cause I ain't just leavin' it here."

Righting it, he dropped the kickstand and began blowing sand from the engine.

"Some grit on the cam chain, an' the exhaust pipe's a little beat up, but that shouldn't be tough to fix."

"Please don't do this."

Anthony shook his head. It would be downright un-American. He'd go into hock to give her a good life, and stay away from other women, but he wasn't going to leave a motorcycle lying in the middle of the desert. He loved her, but he wasn't out of his goddamn mind.

He began walking the bike back to the road. When he reached the shoulder, he slid into the seat.

"Please," Maria said, standing beside him. "There's something wrong with all this. I *feel* it."

He adjusted the clutch, started the bike, and looked at her. He shouted over the din.

"You bein' a Nervous Nellie is all that's wrong. Hey, this bike may be a little old-fashioned, but nothin's gonna happen."

Winking at her, Anthony throttled up and eased onto the road.

The breeze felt good. The speed felt great. Anthony smiled.

As Anthony tore down the road, someone ran in front of him: a child, holding a ragdoll and waving.

She ran out so fast that he wasn't able to avoid her. Hitting the child, he swerved to the right, lost his balance, and tumbled down the embankment.

Screaming, Maria jumped into the car and drove over. Anthony was lying on his belly, blood seeping from tears in his blue jeans and white T-shirt. He was holding his side and moaning.

"*Anthony!* Can you *move?*"

"Chest . . . hurts. Leg . . ."

Racing back to the car, Maria drove it down the embankment, ducked a shoulder under his arm, and slowly, gently helped him up. Laying him in the back seat, she used their suitcases to brace him in place then sped back onto the road and headed west.

All the while, Anthony moaned about a little girl with a doll, wanting to know how she was. His wife frantically insisted that there had been no one else, but he didn't believe her.

A half-hour later, Anthony was on an examining table in Willcox. He had broken three ribs, his left leg, and had suffered a mild concussion. The doctor said he was going to have to be taken to Tucson for proper care.

While Maria waited for an ambulance, she told a police officer how the accident had happened. When she repeated what Anthony had said about a little girl, the man looked at her strangely.

"You sure he said a little girl?"

"With a doll of some kind."

He continued to stare at her.

"But I was watching the whole time," she insisted. "There was no one when he was riding, or when I drove past."

He said quietly, "I'm not surprised."

"You're not?"

"Twenty years ago, a soldier just home from the war got caught up in a bottleneck in Phoenix. He was in a hurry to see his wife, so instead of waiting, he borrowed a bike and took to the road. Ran down a little girl while her father fixed a flat tire. No one was to blame; the kid just ran out. She and the GI both died. We left the motorcycle there, but it was gone when we went back. Every year since then, on the anniversary of the accident, someone reports seeing *something* out there, one of the victims or the bike or both. But this is the first time we've had someone actually get *on* the vehicle." He shook his head. "I never saw anything myself, but I always wondered about it. I guess those of us who were there the first time don't *need* to see it again."

Folding away his notebook and tipping his hat, he headed toward the door.

"Take this as a warning, ma'am. Very few folks ever get a second chance at life."

Anthony recovered, and, back in Mamaroneck, he spent as much time talking to local kids about driver safety as he did fixing cars.

Neither the little girl nor the motorcycle was ever seen again. They had found their apostle.

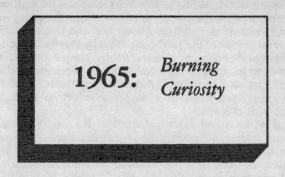

# 1965: *Burning Curiosity*

It was July 14, and it ended the longest wait of Dr. Brian Boyd's life.

Along with a manned landing on the moon, which was still at least four years off, the exploration of Mars was one of NASA's top priorities. And now, after a 228-day, 325-million-mile journey, the hardy *Mariner IV* space probe was about to reach the mysterious Red Planet. The probe's flyby would beam back the first close-up pictures of the world, pictures unobscured by the thick and shifting atmosphere of Earth. Pictures which would allow scientists to see details on the surface of the planet for the first time.

Yet, as he drove to the Jet Propulsion Laboratory in Pasadena, California, Dr. Boyd had mixed feelings about the approaching event.

The scientist had grown up with all the great literature about the fourth planet from the sun. With H. G. Wells's

*War of the Worlds.* With the epic Mars novels of Edgar Rice Burroughs. With the countless tales spun in the pages of magazines such as *Amazing, Astounding,* and *Galaxy.* And with a ratty copy of the 1905 book *Mars* by Percival Lowell, the astronomer who had inadvertently started the Mars craze when he mapped the planet's canals, popularizing the notion that what he called highly advanced "Martian folk" had constructed them in a desperate effort to avert a planet-wide drought.

The stories about Mars had inspired the young boy to become a scientist specializing in planetary geology. And now, *Mariner IV* was about to tell them once and for all whether the Mars of fiction was also the Mars of fact. Dr. Boyd had even placed his old copy of Lowell's *Mars* in his briefcase, just to have it with him, to hold it in his hands after events had rendered it a work of unparalleled prophecy or of wide-eyed fantasy.

Dr. Boyd joined his colleagues at the *Mariner* command center, then waited for the data to come in. It was the small hours of July 15 before the pictures began to arrive. Actually, they were hundreds of thousands of numbers corresponding to sixty-four varying shades of black, white, and gray, which a computer on Earth reconstructed as photographs.

The first picture was dim, a few dark smudges on a plain; the image could be anything. Not so with later pictures. Dr. Boyd was fascinated, but crushed. The Martian surface showed no canals, but jagged mountains, craters, and valleys. Mars was not a world of beings struggling to build huge irrigation ditches; it was a planet more like our own moon, rocky and apparently quite dead.

There were congratulations all around as data continued to arrive. Dr. Boyd joined in, proud of the achievement of the JPL team. But the boy in him was numb.

When all twenty-two pictures had come in, each one showing vistas similar in their desolation, Dr. Boyd went to his office where he sat in the dark, hands steepled in front of his mouth, the copy of *Mars* sitting before him. Strangely, he ached for the memory of Percival Lowell. The author had shaped a generation of science fiction and of space scientists who had a touch of the romantic. Over the course of the next few days, as the photographs were published and as their impact sank in, the magic would die.

The astronomer dreaded to think what would happen to the space program when men finally landed on the moon and didn't find Wells's Selenites or Burroughs's Moon Men or any green cheese. All of this was wonderful fodder for the scientists, but there would be nothing to fire the imagination of the public.

As Dr. Boyd sat there, he felt a presence that was as real yet as fleeting as *déjà vu*. A moment later, the cover of the old book flew open to the frontispiece, a print of Lowell's Mars. He stared at it for a moment, then rolled his chair over and closed the book.

It popped open again.

Scowling, the astronomer riffled through the pages, looking to see if something were lodged inside. There was nothing, and he shut the cover again.

It flipped up.

Dr. Boyd sat still, waiting to see if he'd somehow failed to feel an earth tremor. Nothing else moved, and no one else was shouting about an earthquake. He leaned over, picked up the book, and held it in front of him.

Much to his surprise, it was softly shaking, *upward,* and when he set it down, the cover opened again. The pages fluttered, past the tissue-paper insert which covered the picture of Mars, past the print itself, to the text beyond.

Dr. Boyd looked around. The windows were all shut, the air conditioning didn't seem to be acting up, and there was nothing strange happening to anything else in the room. He had a weird thought, and was tempted to call a fellow astronomer in Hawaii, to see if anything strange was happening to *his* copy of *Mars;* he refrained, knowing how ridiculous it would sound.

The book stopped moving and, suddenly, he heard something moving behind him. He felt a weight on his shoulder, a hand, and it squeezed him firmly.

Then there was a voice, and it said softly, "A new generation will see the photographs and wonder about them, just as your generation wondered about the *canali.* As long as there is a curious mind, the sense of wonder will never die."

Boyd spun around, but there was nothing. He rubbed his face, looked again, and sank back in his chair.

Was it possible? Had some other world sent Lowell here, data bit by data bit, like the pictures from Mars?

He smiled, feeling a bit silly.

The ghost of an old astronomer. Really!

The scientist in him rejected the thought. He'd imagined it all. People died. What was important, though, was that his little vision had been correct: wonder and imagination would live always.

Then he noticed the book, and his smile faded.

Something had been underlined in pencil, a passage in a discussion about the resilience of the human animal:

"Mind has been his making."

Beneath it, also written in pencil, were the initials "P.L."

# 1967: *Funny Books*

"Cap" Sherman grew up immersed in a singularly American art form: the comic book.

A child of the Depression, Cap would hide behind the local newsstand reading the latest *Captain Marvel* or *Human Torch* comic until the vendor saw him and chased him away. When he wasn't at school or working in his father's butcher shop, Cap wrote and drew his own comics.

As an adult, he talked a printer into advancing him money to publish his own line of comic books. The magazines made their debut in the late 1950s and were a huge success.

A decade later, Cap decided to merge one American art form with another. Iconoclastic rock-'n'-roll was a hit on the airwaves and in the record stores, and feeling a comic book would do equally as well, he signed singer-songwriter Randy Wick to write him a bunch of stories.

The scripts Wick turned in were poetic but somewhat esoteric. Fearing that younger kids might not be able to follow them, Cap asked Wick to stop by the office after-hours for a chat.

It was nearly eight before the rock-'n'-roller showed up.

"Sorry," Wick said, not bothering to remove his sunglasses. He looked out the open sixth-floor window, shuddered, then flopped on the sofa. He pulled a joint from a pocket of his beaded jacket. "I got held up."

"You look like shit."

"Feel like it."

"Luckily, you don't write like it."

"Thanks, man."

"But we *do* have a little problem."

"In a minute, man."

Wick lit the cigarette, drew on it, then passed it across the desk to Cap. The publisher took a long drag.

"Whoa!"

"Good, huh?"

"Stee-*rong!*"

"Hey, you only live once. Might as well do it first class." Wick chuckled as he pulled his ponytail over his shoulder and toyed with it. "So, what's this little problem?"

"We need something to reach the kids."

"Bull. Let them reach us."

"Well, yes. But we've got to *help* them."

"Groovy. Sell Monarch Notes."

Cap tried to focus as the smoke hit him. "I have another suggestion. A small one. You've got all the band members in your stories quoting Kafka and Descartes."

"Like I said, first class."

"Yes. But I have *another* first-class idea. Why not have them quote other rock-'n'-rollers?"

"Like?"

"You tell me."

"Only Dylan, Lennon, and me are worth quoting."

"Fine. Then quote the three of you."

"But kids already know what we have to say."

"This will give them a fresh outlook—"

The phone rang, and Cap picked up while Wick mulled over the suggestion.

"Cap Comics."

"Hello, is Mr. Cap Sherman there?"

"Speaking."

"Sir, this is Inspector Jacob Varley, Midtown South. I believe you know a Randy Wick."

Cap's eyes narrowed as he looked at the rocker. "Yes."

"I'd like to stop by and talk to you about him."

"What did he do, Inspector? Disturb the neighbors?"

"No. He just died, Mr. Sherman."

Cap felt sick. Wick continued to play with his ponytail.

"Who is this?" Cap demanded.

"Sir?"

"Is this some kind of joke?"

"Not unless you have a morbid sense of humor, sir. Mr. Wick was in his apartment and was using LSD—he took a walk out his window."

"Inspector, it can't be rock singer Randy Wick you're talking about. Mr. Wick is here with me."

"If he is, you're hallucinating too. Mr. Wick was just scraped off West Eighth Street. His girlfriend was with him. I'd like to come by and take a statement regarding anything you know about his use of drugs, where he might have gotten them, whom he associated with, that sort of thing."

Cap continued to stare at Wick. "This can't be true."

"It is, sir. You're in the Taub Building?"

"Yes."

"I'll be there in ten minutes."

"I'll wait for you," Cap said numbly, and let the phone slide back into its cradle. He looked over at Wick.

"Randy, what's going on?"

Wick shrugged slightly. "It's like the man said."

"I don't believe it."

"Believe it."

Wick reached up. He lowered his sunglasses slightly and peered over the top.

"It's a gas," Wick said, peering out with eyes that had rolled back into his head and were solid white. "A perpetual high."

Cap bolted from behind his desk.

He had intended to go to the stairwell, but the grass left

him dizzy. He got as far as his office door before he collapsed on the carpet.

Wick walked over and Cap managed to look up. The side of the rocker's head was caved in, and blood was running down his jacket.

"For the record," Wick said, "I thought I was walking out the goddamn bathroom door."

Cap passed out.

The publisher came to when someone slapped him on the cheek.

"You all right, Mr. Sherman?"

Cap opened his eyes. He saw a man who he assumed was Inspector Varley. A uniformed officer was standing behind him.

"Yeah, I think so."

Cap got his hands under him and made it to his knees. He looked around. Sniffed. The open window had swept away the smell of the pot.

No one would believe him. He tried to stand, and the inspector helped him up.

"Take it from one who's guilty of the same thing," Varley said, "you're working too hard. I've never seen dead men alive and I've never fainted, but I've seen a face that looks like yours. Take a day off."

Varley settled Cap into the sofa, and the publisher dragged a hand across his face.

Maybe he *had* imagined the whole thing. The pot? It could have been his own stuff. Maybe he'd smoked that while waiting for Wick and dreamed up the rest of it.

That's when he noticed the comic book scripts on his desk.

Wincing because he got up too fast, Cap staggered over and riffled through the pages.

Every one of them had been edited, in handwriting that was not his. The quotes, from Dylan, Lennon, and mostly from Wick, were ones he wouldn't have known.

Cap never said anything about the pages to anyone, nor did he ever publish the comic book. He still thought it was a terrific idea, which is why he cancelled it.

He didn't want Wick coming back for a second issue.

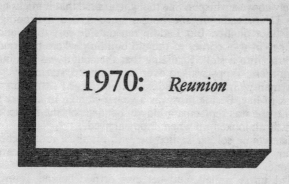

# 1970: *Reunion*

For years, the Johnsons knew that their family farm in Westminster, Maryland, was haunted.

It began when their new dog Laddie started acting strangely. A collie, he would sit at sunset and follow objects in rooms or outside—objects which weren't there. When the vet came to look at the other animals, Wade Johnson also had him check the dog. There was nothing wrong with the animal, physically, though much to everyone's surprise, the docile collie nipped at the vet, something he'd never done before.

Something in the air, something unseen, was making him skittish.

As the weeks passed, Laddie became more and more agitated at sundown, barking and even snapping at family members. When Wade Johnson was beginning to think he might have to put the animal to sleep, his fourteen-year-old daughter, Tappy, saw just what was bothering the animal.

Out in the barn early one evening, she heard a voice,

barely above a whisper. She thought, at first, that it might be the TV or radio in the house, since it had a droning, indistinct quality. But Laddie ran outside just then, and went right to a corner of the old building, where he stood barking into a stall. Realizing that the sound was coming from there, Tappy walked over, and stopped, staring.

A man wearing a Confederate uniform was sitting on a stack of hay. Beside him was a young woman in a nurse's outfit; she was replacing a bloody bandage on the soldier's arm. Both looked up when Tappy arrived.

The young soldier smiled beneath his thick moustache. "E'en," he said softly. "We haven't been meanin' to scare anyone."

The nurse smiled, and her eyes drifted behind Tappy. Someone coughed.

"How is my patient?"

Tappy turned. Laddie was sitting on his haunches, growling at a portly gentleman in a white suit. The older gentleman was carrying a medical bag.

"He's mending," the woman said.

The soldier was still looking at Tappy. "Every year," he said, "as it gets closer, we come back."

"As what gets closer?" Tappy asked.

"The anniversary of the fire," said the old doctor. "We were here, trying to get home to Virginia, when the Yankees chased us just for fun. Major Custis, here, left his unit and tried to help."

"They shot him," the nurse said.

"And when they found us in here," the doctor said, "the blasted blue bast—, er, the Northerners burned the barn down. And us with it."

"We didn't survive," the soldier said.

Tappy looked from one to the other. "I don't believe you."

"Look up the Custis family in Richmond," the doctor suggested. "Or my own brood, the Fosters. You'll believe us then."

"I can't believe this. I'm talking to—ghosts. But you're not evil."

"No, miss. The living are far more cruel."

"We don't understand any of this either," Major Custis went on. "We all remember the smoke, passing out. Someone rebuilt the barn, and now we seem to *sleep*, without dreaming, until it's time for us to come back."

"We talk about it every year," the doctor said. "We think it has to do with dying before our time. Being murdered. St. Peter wasn't ready for us, so we ended up in a kind of in-between world. Our guess is it happens to many folk."

The floorboards creaked in the loft. The soldier and nurse looked up. The dog stopped his growling, and stepped back, whimpering.

The doctor came up beside Tappy. "Like him."

"Like who?"

"That one. Whoever's up there. You see, we aren't here alone. Even during those terrible days we were here hiding, we felt something. A *presence*."

Upstairs, the hay door rattled.

"Maybe it wants to get out," Tappy said.

"That's very possible," the doctor said. "We figure that some people just can't accept their fate."

"Did you ever go up there?"

"When we were hiding," the major said, "we dared not leave here. And now, we can't."

Tappy looked back at the dog. Laddie was still whining, wanting no part of whatever was upstairs. The young girl turned from the group and went to the ladder.

"Miss," the doctor called as she started up, "do be careful. I can't practice my healing arts on anyone except the major."

Tappy nodded and continued up. She had done this hundreds of times during her life, yet now it was as if she were seeing everything for the first time. Hearing the rungs squeak, noticing the thickness of the shadows, feeling the isolation.

The last of the sun's rays crept around the door. As her head reached the level of the loft, Tappy looked around. She saw nothing but the hay and tools outlined ever so gently in orange.

The door rattled again. Tappy gazed at it, allowing her eyes to adjust to the greater darkness up here.

She saw two large eyes, barely rimmed in white. As she watched, a long muzzle seemed to materialize from the darkness. A gray shape, like that of a wolf, was glaring at her.

There was a trace of blood on its mouth, and more on its side. It had probably been feeding in the old barn when it was shot; how many years ago, and by whom, she couldn't begin to imagine.

The animal threw itself against the door again, then snarled with rage.

"It's a wolf!" she shouted down. "Dare I let it go?"

"It cannot go. Neither can we. This is our perdition, miss."

Feeling a sickness unlike any she had ever experienced, Tappy backed down the ladder. She walked slowly to the stall; when she arrived, the ghosts were gone. Laddie was walking around inside, sniffing.

Tappy brought her father and mother to the barn the next night, and the ghosts returned. When the elder Johnsons got over the initial shock, the family and their guests had a pleasant, albeit strange, conversation. The ghosts remained for three days more—ten in all—before vanishing for the rest of that year.

The wolf returned too, though after Wade Johnson went up to have a look at it, no one ever returned at night.

Tappy wondered how many other spirits walked their land, walked the earth itself, unseen and unsuspected on the anniversary of their untimely death.

Strangely, though, not even on that first night did the specters frighten her. On the contrary. The promise of an afterlife, however different from any she'd imagined, filled the young girl with wonder and hope.

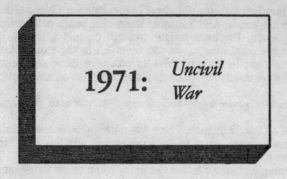

**1971:** *Uncivil War*

The power was back, and Preston thanked God. He could see *McCloud*.

Not that the show mattered much. The twenty-eight-year-old carpenter would have watched *The Don Knotts Show*—anything was better than sitting at home on a summer night with nothing to do. Which was exactly what he'd been doing since the violent thunderstorm hit Johnston County, North Carolina, over an hour before. Preston had recently moved up from a shack in Louisiana. For the duration of the blackout, all he had done was sit in his armchair muttering that he might as well have stayed there, living off his old generator, if this was the best the city could do when the weather turned bad.

Then the power came on again, just in time for the show. Preston grabbed a bag of pretzels and settled down in front of his new color set.

Thunder crashed somewhere in the distance. Outside, the skies darkened. And a minute later, rain began pelting the roof again. Preston's mouth twisted; he had a feeling it wasn't a good idea to get too involved in the story. Sure enough, the lights and TV went out, then came on again; they were steady for a moment, then snapped off and stayed off.

Preston swore again and slumped deeper into the armchair.

Of all the damn luck. There was nothing to do now but sit here and mope, or go to the window and watch it rain. He opted for the rain.

Dragging himself across the living room of his four-room home, Preston pulled up the blinds and stared out at the downpour. It always amazed him how lightning could make a place look like it was noon. Whenever it flashed, he looked across the field behind his house, trying to make out as many familiar objects as he could. He noticed that there were lights on in the new housing development at the other end of the field. It was just his luck to be tied to an old power station which crapped out during storms.

The next flash revealed something odd: there seemed to be people on the field, a crowd of them. Preston held his head steady and didn't blink, in order to see them better when the next bolt ripped the skies.

He did, but he didn't believe what he saw.

There were men out there: Union and Confederate soldiers locked in battle.

Pulling off his shoes and socks, Preston ran outside, crossing the wet grass with giant strides, shielding his eyes as he peered through the sheets of rain.

Now he could hear the men yelling, mingled with the roar of gun and cannon fire. Whenever lightning flashed, he could see the men clearly. They were fighting. Horses galloped, some riderless; men fought at a distance and at close range, many with sabers clanging.

When Preston neared the battle, he suddenly stopped, concerned lest it was real ammunition they were using. He stopped a few hundred yards away and, drenched, just watched.

The blues and the grays seemed almost the same washed-out color. He could smell the gunpowder. Men were falling and dying. *Really* dying. The red of the blood stood out quite clearly. So did the cries of pain, the moans of dying men.

This was nuts. Where had these people come from? What were they doing here?

Then it occurred to him: perhaps they'd never left. The thought caused him to tense, and Preston turned and ran back to the house, making the sign of the cross as he splashed through deep puddles, wondering if he were going to be struck by lightning for having witnessed something that was quite possibly profane. Down in Louisiana, he thought he'd seen a swamp creature once. But that couldn't have been a *real* supernatural event. That had made him snicker; not this. This scared the breath out of him.

As he ran, he tried to decide whom he was going to call when he got back to the house: the police or a priest. He decided on the former. At least he was sure they'd make a house call.

Dialing the number, Preston made his report, then stood by the window and watched. The storm was passing, but not the vision. In the faint bolts shining through the clouds, he could see the two armies still clashing.

The police arrived in just over five minutes. An older officer came to the door, and seemed disinterested as Preston pulled him to the window while breathlessly explaining what he'd seen.

The last of the thunderstorm was grumbling near the horizon as the officer stood by the window. He didn't bother looking out.

Preston looked at him. "You don't believe me," he said forlornly.

"Oh, I believe ya," the officer said. "I jest don't know why the dispatcher didn't tell ya himself what it was ya saw."

"You mean—other people have seen it?"

"Many times, always durin' an' after a storm. What it is is our beloved General Joseph E. Johnston and ol' William T. Sherman fightin' their battle over and over." The officer looked outside as the last of the ghostly figures faded. "The investigators who've been here call it a 'vile vortex,' but I always felt the earth was answerin' the heavens the only way it could, with a battle that was as loud and deadly as nature's fury itself." He smiled, patted Preston on the shoulder, then started toward the door. "Now if you'll excuse me, I've got to explain this all again to a couple o' folks livin' on the other side of the field."

Preston eventually got used to the idea that there were ghosts living in his backyard. In the years which followed, the power would fail often during summer storms. When it did, Preston wouldn't complain. Even when it didn't, he would shut off the TV and lights, go to his window, and stare out, unblinking, as lightning lit the field. Only on rare occasions would the ghosts appear, replaying the battle the same way each time. Yet as many times as he looked out on the field, and regardless of what he saw, he never grew bored, nor failed to look on with a sense of wonder.

**1972:** *The
Phantom
Returns*

It's a situation unique in all of Hollywood.

On the lot of Universal Studios in Universal City, California, stands a soundstage which still contains the magnificent set for the Lon Chaney Sr. film classic *The Phantom of the Opera.* The opera stage, and all of the magnificent boxes which surround it, remain as they were when they were built in 1925. Other sets are constructed inside the opera set—but the Chaney set itself has never been dismantled.

Nor is anyone likely to try.

Universal produced many of the greatest horror films in history—not just the Chaney films, but also *Dracula, Frankenstein, The Wolf Man, The Mummy,* and their many sequels. Thus, film historian Dan Stevens, from St. Louis, was anxious to see the studio before beginning work on a book about horror films.

Fortunately, his cousin, Judith Graff, was a guide on the Universal tour. She was able to get him permission to see the opera set on the part of the lot the public wasn't permitted to visit—that portion where the films are actually made.

Meeting at the Lankershim Boulevard gate when Judith got off at seven, she and Dan strolled back, past the bungalows where the stars and producers have their offices, toward the soundstages. Judith was busy complaining about how a tram had broken down in front of the *Psycho* house, and she'd had trouble convincing tourists that the breakdown was real and not part of a fright show of some kind. Dan hadn't realized that the classic Hitchcock facade was still standing, and asked if he could see it after visiting the Chaney stage. Judith offered to book him a room there.

The sun was setting, and in the fading light the cadaverous face of the Phantom, painted atop a wall of the soundstage, seemed especially menacing. It thrilled Dan to think that this was where film history had been made, and that the accountants who ran the studio had actually had the sensitivity to save this magnificent piece of that history.

Crews had already finished the day's work on a set which was being built for a film. Naked plywood boards were beginning to resemble someone's bedroom, but Dan didn't dwell on that. When Judith switched on the lights, the splendor of the opera set drew his complete attention.

She chatted like a tour guide, telling him about how down through the years workers had complained of being bothered by electric tools which shut down inexplicably, props and lights being overturned, scripts disappearing. Some even claimed to have seen Lon Chaney lurking in the wings, making certain that his set was not harmed.

Of course they had, he said, given the way drugs and drink abound in Hollywood. He shook his head, lamenting the lost days of the film industry's real glory. The days when Lon Chaney and Charlie Chaplin and Douglas Fairbanks Sr. were kings—when people made movies because they loved the medium, not just the money.

The set was smaller than it had seemed in the film, even claustrophobic. But that didn't detract from it. He turned around, looking in all directions, remembering the camera angles, imagining the silent film crew at work, trying to picture the horror maestro himself, Lon Chaney, the Man of a Thousand Faces, standing off in the shadows, getting into the character of the tortured musician who lived in the catacombs beneath the opera house.

He was about to ask Judith if he could go onto the stage when one of the bedroom walls fell backwards. It hit the ground with a *whuuump*, and the two people jumped back, nearly onto Lankershim.

When she caught her breath, Judith swore. She'd been standing near it and had nearly been flattened. She asked Dan to help her lift it, and propped it back up with the sandbag which had somehow slipped away. She told Dan to hurry before something else got wrecked.

Deciding to go onstage, Dan walked briskly ahead, grumbling at how a set nearly fifty years old held up better than one just fifty minutes old. Like the shabby quality of today's horror films, it was a dismal sign of the times.

Then the lights went out.

Dan froze, afraid he'd bump into something. Judith asked if he'd tripped over a cord or something, but he told her no. Then she called out, convinced that someone else from the tour had set this up to scare them. No one answered.

She told him to stand still, that she was going to try to feel her way to one of the doors. Then she muttered how if anything else broke down on a horror set today she was going to get out of this business and become a waitress.

While Dan stood there, the fallen plywood wall creaked, as though someone were walking across it. Judith had to be right. Someone *was* having cruel fun with them.

A moment later, something brushed the back of Dan's left hand. Having expected something like that, he made a quick grab to that side; he came up empty.

He listened, expecting to hear footsteps. There were none. Whoever touched him had stopped.

That would be their downfall.

There hadn't been anything in front of him and, spreading his arms, he took a large step forward, hoping to grab the joker behind all of this.

He gave a triumphant cry as his arms closed around a figure. It giggled.

Judith.

She pulled out her tourguide flashlight, shined it at her face, and grinned. She said she couldn't resist, not with his interest in monsters.

He nodded good-naturedly; a moment later, the plywood creaked again. The young woman stopped grinning.

Dan asked if it were a friend of hers. She shook her head as she shined the flashlight towards the plywood. There was no one near the fallen wall, and she pushed the beam around the soundstage.

The flashlight died.

Judith said she was going to turn on the lights, her voice trailing behind as she hurried off, feeling her way. Dan remained where he was, not quite convinced that this wasn't part of her gag, or that of Judith's coworkers.

He suddenly began to detect a musty smell which seemed to come from his left. It grew stronger and then was directly in front of him, the dry dust causing his nostrils to clog. He reached out and felt nothing, yet he knew someone was there. He sensed a weight, a presence; he felt eyes watching him.

Then the lights came back on, and for a moment, from their different places on the soundstage, both Dan and Judith saw a human shadow move across the floor. It rose up onto the stage, went behind the proscenium, and vanished, along with the odor.

The two young people stood there for a long moment, looking at each other, before Judith suggested that they leave.

Dan's curiosity nearly drove him to go to the stage to have a look around—nearly, but not quite. He opted to join Judith at the door, concluding that he would much prefer to see the shadow of Lon Chaney on the screen, not on the floor.

They skipped the *Psycho* house and went to a nice, bright restaurant for dinner.

A presence has been felt or seen on the soundstage many times since—several times, in fact, when a horror film, *The Cat People,* was filmed there in 1982. However, it was never again felt by Judith, who gave up being a tourguide and now sells insurance.

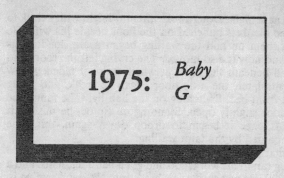

# 1975: *Baby G*

For the few days that the wraith haunted the small, unassuming home of the Masons in Parkland, Washington, outside of Tacoma, it caused the kind of suffering not usually associated with ghosts. Afraid, at first, mechanical engineer Doug Mason learned that there was more to a haunting than disembodied voices in the night.

The couple first became aware of the ghost when they heard crying in the middle of the night. The high, hollow wail came from the foot of the bed. When Mason turned on the light, the crying stopped, but resumed shortly after he turned it off. His wife Linda was able to sleep with the pillow pulled over her head, and their two daughters heard nothing, but Doug slept fitfully.

The next day, after work, Doug checked the room for open windows or cracks through which the wind could have come whistling. He found none, and hoped the noise had been a fluke.

It wasn't.

The next night, Doug awoke after midnight with a chill, to find the blankets bunched on the floor beside his wife. He pulled them on and the wailing began again, louder this time, and now it also moved. The crying left the room and stopped beneath the attic, at which point it faded. A few moments later, the attic door began to creak, and Doug bolted from bed. Switching on the hall light, he found the attic door slightly open. Standing on tiptoe, he pushed it shut. At once it began to droop down again, this time accompanied by the faint wailing.

So that was it, he thought: a wind in the attic.

Doug ran to his workshop and got a hammer, nails, and a step stool. He whacked a few brads into the door, sealing it, then went back to bed.

He was nearly asleep when he heard an unmistakable groaning sound as the nails were wrenched from the wood. Jumping out of bed, he found the door hanging open and the wailing coming, now, from the attic.

Common sense told him there was an intruder, but the sounds had definitely come from the bedroom. Maybe it was a Paul Winchell?

The thought of being robbed by a ventriloquist amused him as he lowered the steps from inside the door and cautiously ascended. Tugging on the light, he poked his head through the opening and looked in.

The crying stopped. The bare bulb illuminated old toys, suitcases, and boxes of clothing. He climbed in, poised on his hands and knees, and looked around. The only thing that had been disturbed was a carton of the girls' old baby clothes, which were strewn across the back of the attic.

Baby clothes, and a cry which could have been that of a small child. It couldn't have been a prowler, but Doug didn't like what he was thinking. He left quickly.

The next day, during lunch, he went to the local newspaper office to find out if there had ever been any reports, locally, of strange voices or disturbances, especially involving clothing or beds. As it happened, one journalist, a young woman named Alaine, had reported on local poltergeists when she edited her college newspaper in Seattle. Talking about the subject as if it were an everyday event, she said that there *was* a spirit which fit the bill: the ghost of little Jeannie Cleveland.

In 1896, she explained, Lucas Cleveland, his wife Merry, and four-year-old Jeannie set out for Seattle from Oregon en route to the Yukon, where Lucas hoped to make a killing during the gold rush. The child took ill and didn't survive the journey. She was buried in an unmarked grave somewhere in Seattle. Lucas died a year later, in a flood, and his wife returned to Oregon.

Jeannie's ghost was first seen when Merry died in 1910. She was only heard for a day or two, then she began to materialize at night, wandering naked through the hotel in Seattle where she had lain ill. The manager and a housekeeper both had seen her crying for her mother and pulling blankets from beds in order to stay warm.

When he heard about the blankets, Doug felt sick.

Alaine reported that the child departed the hotel after a week. Sometime later, she showed up along a roadside in Tacoma and in other places, always moving south, as though heading home, calling for her mother. Her last known appearance had occurred over nine years before.

Doug was a religious man, and his initial fear gave way to pity. He wondered if there were anything that could be done to help the spirit. Alaine said she had some ideas about that, and offered to sleep at the Mason home in order to try them out. Doug agreed.

Alaine came to dinner that night, and after a few hours of backgammon with the Mason girls she bedded down on the living room sofa. Doug had spent the time working on something Alaine had suggested he prepare: a gravestone with the little girl's name on it. He made it out of wood, using a stencil to paint her name.

Doug had trouble falling asleep that night, troubled by thoughts of the poor girl. At 1:10 in the morning, still awake, he heard the youthful voice calling again from the hallway.

"Mama? Mama, hold me, I'm so cold!"

Doug ran out, followed by his wife. They were met by Alaine, who stood on the opposite end of the corridor, a cassette recorder in one hand, her blanket in the other. Between them, a hazy blob of light hovered just above the floor.

"Jeannie?" said Alaine.

"Mama?"

Linda freaked and ran back into the bedroom. Alaine and Doug walked closer to the glow. It was metamorphosing, beginning to take on features—arms, legs, and a head. The voice was definitely coming from inside the apparition.

"No," Alaine said, "it's a friend of Mama's. Are you cold?"

"Yes."

"Come to me, then. I'll warm you."

Slowly, the reporter set the recorder down and held open the blanket. The light started moving toward her.

Doug watched without fear, but with a sense of sadness so profound he had difficulty breathing. The voice was plaintive, pitiful, the more so because it seemed so helpless.

"Where are you?" Alaine asked as the light came nearer, now clearly the image of a little girl.

"In the ground."

"Where, my love?"

"By a pretty stream."

"You like streams?"

"Yes. We had one near our home. Do you know where my home is?"

"Yes," Alaine said. "Yes, I do."

There were tears in the reporter's eyes as the girl came toward the blanket. With each step she took, she seemed to fade a little. Then, a smile on her face as she snuggled into the blanket, she vanished. The cover collapsed on the floor.

Doug and Alaine didn't wait until morning to do what they had to do. Going to her car, they set out for Seattle, listening to the tape on the way up, hearing everything which had transpired.

In her research, Alaine had discovered where the Clevelands had stayed in Seattle. Though the hotel was no longer there, not far away there *was* a stream. They went to it.

Uncertain quite what to do, they dug a shallow hole, placed the blanket inside, lay the tombstone on top of it, and then covered the hole again. They said a short prayer before leaving.

The voice never returned to the Mason household, nor to

anywhere else. But on quiet nights, on the small river which runs from Puget Sound just south of the city, people have said that more than the running water can sometimes be heard. They say it sounds almost like the contented sighs of a young child—a child who, nearly eighty years after her death, finally found peace.

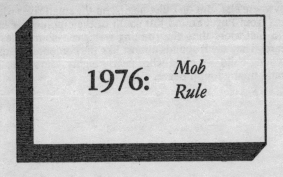

# 1976: *Mob Rule*

When thirty-two-year-old Nate Smith moved from Miami to Chicago in October to take a job managing a department store, he knew nothing about the Windy City. Nearly two months later, he still didn't.

An agent had found him his quaint, old apartment, and it was a bargain; he took the bus to work, found a small grocery store a short walk away, and learned where the movie theaters and restaurants were, which was all the recreation he had time for.

However, he *did* experience a part of the city few people knew, or would want to know.

Late in November, when he'd leave for work some mornings, Nate would find the front door unlocked. He never left it open at night, and was confounded—until he noticed that it happened only when he left the adjoining hall closet door slightly ajar.

The landlord replaced the lock, but that didn't cause the problem to go away; the solution, obviously and inexplicably, was to keep the closet door shut.

A few days after this phenomenon began, Nate started finding lipstick on his drinking glass when he'd come home at night. The cleaning woman didn't wear lipstick, and no one else had his new key. More puzzling, however, was that nothing was ever taken from the apartment. Even when he left a five-dollar bill on the counter, he returned home to find it where he'd placed it.

However, nothing truly disconcerting happened to Nate until he was at home on Thanksgiving Day.

A turkey was in the oven, the parade was on TV, and he had the strongest feeling that he was being watched. He happened to notice that the closet door was open. When he walked over and shut it, the feeling left him.

Calling the landlord, Nate inquired if there might be a shaft or pipe or anything behind it that could cause it to generate heat or cold or vibrations or anything that might affect the rest of the house. The landlord said no. The apartment was solidly built, and he couldn't see a lock being *shaken* open.

That also wouldn't explain the lipstick on the glass, Nate knew, assuming the two things were related.

Nate asked the landlord about the previous residents of the apartment. The landlord told him it had been unoccupied for several years, but he had no idea why, since he'd only been here two years himself.

Nate sat down in the living room and tried to enjoy the parade. He failed. His eyes were continually drawn to the closet.

Curious, he opened it again and sat back down. The feeling that he was being watched quickly returned. He shut it again.

Pacing more from frustration than anything else, he decided to go next door and have a chat with his neighbors, the Marxes. He'd met them in the elevator several times, and Mrs. Marx had invited him to dinner; but his hours were such that he'd never taken her up on the offer.

The elderly couple welcomed him, and sitting down with

a cup of coffee, Nate asked them what they knew about the previous tenants.

"Nothing," Mr. Marx replied, "except that they were a young couple."

"They always did seem nervous," Mrs. Marx said.

"The times, I guess," commented Mr. Marx.

Nate asked if they had any idea where the couple went; he was told that they'd left Chicago.

Declining an invitation to stay for dinner, Nate went back to his apartment.

He opened the closet door.

The feeling returned, but he rode with it. It grew more intense. Soon, Nate no longer had just a sense of being watched: he felt as though someone was in the room with him.

There wasn't; at least, no one that he could see. But he felt a presence, utterly still but aware, a damp and living *something*.

He wondered if it might be a mouse. Or several. Or a nest of cockroaches. But then there was the lock, and the lipstick.

The sensation grew stronger, causing the small of his back to tingle. He got up to shut the door, but stopped, staring at it. He saw something in the dark.

Crouching forward, he approached cautiously, cursing himself silently for having forgotten to buy a flashlight. All he needed was to have something jump out at him. His life would end, on the spot.

Whatever was in the closet was foul, he could smell it now. Like the cat that had had a litter in the wall insulation of a store he'd managed. The kittens were stuck there and they all died, stinking like nothing he could have imagined.

Until now.

He took small, wary steps, squinting into the dark—and then he saw it.

A woman.

There was a handkerchief tied round her mouth, and blood oozing from dark holes in her dress. She'd been shot, but she was still alive: her eyes were open and staring, imploring.

"Dear Lord!"

Nate ran forward and reached gently for the gag. But he ended up with only the hem of his coat in his hand.

The woman was gone.

He rose, his legs shaking, heart slamming in his chest. Looking at his coat, he suddenly pushed his hand into a pocket, pulled out his agent's crumpled business card, and called her at home.

He apologized for interrupting her family get-together, but he had to know if anyone was ever killed in his apartment.

The woman laughed, "Oh, there've been rumors. The building has a fascinating history. I'd have told you if you weren't so busy. Gangsters had rooms there in the twenties and thirties, and many kept ladies there. Who knows what might have happened when a girl got a little too big for her nylons?"

Nate thanked her, poured himself a brandy, and sat back down in front of the TV. The Superman balloon looked big and goofy—just what he needed to help him relax.

Nate wasn't superstitious, and he wasn't about to be chased from his apartment by an apparition. But the following day, he *did* bring a coat rack home from the store, and used it for the years he remained at the apartment.

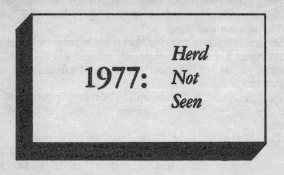

1977:  *Herd*
*Not*
*Seen*

Snowmass, Colorado, lies fifteen miles northwest of Aspen, surrounded and punctuated by the monumental peaks of the Sawatch Range. The heart of the range is accessible by a narrow dirt road which leaves the small town and heads west; few people ever use it, though, unless they're out camping or riding in the foothills. There's nothing here but the magnificent scenery, or so most people believe.

Aspen was growing, and Old Snowmass was a logical place for contractors to turn. The rich could afford and would certainly desire the open tracts of land here, expanses which afforded privacy and scenery.

Surveyor Keith Barnett had grown up in neighboring Basalt, and was hired by local landowners to mark off boundaries in the foothills. With his childhood friend and assistant, Ward, he drove out on a wickedly cold winter morning to begin the project.

The men spent the better part of the day with their theodolite and plumb, marking off hundred-acre-plus parcels, even staying when the weather turned nasty. Only when it began to snow, and their vision was obscured, was it necessary to turn back.

Returning to the pickup, the men drove across the hard, lumpy ground toward the equally hard and lumpy dirt road. Nearly there, the pickup stopped suddenly, flinging the men against the dashboard. It took a moment for them to reorient themselves.

"What'd ya do, hit a rock?" Ward asked.

"I didn't see anything," Keith said as he got out.

Wincing from the bite of the wind, he went around to the front of the vehicle. The grille was smacked in, although he saw nothing around which could have caused it.

He returned to the cab, shaking his head, and started out again.

The vehicle hadn't gone more than a few yards when something hit it again.

"Must be somethin' wrong with the engine," Ward said, and got out with Keith. They lifted the hood, looked inside, saw nothing amiss. There was another loud thump, from somewhere beyond the engine.

"Worst case o' knock I ever saw," Ward said, and went to check around back.

"Holy shit."

"What?"

"Come look."

Keith slogged through the gathering snow and looked to where Ward was pointing: the passenger's door had a huge dent in it which wasn't there before.

"Hail?" Ward asked.

Both men looked around on the ground, saw nothing.

"*Hell's* more like it," Keith said, though he was more concerned than his tone suggested.

They got back in and started slowly toward the road; the vehicle knocked again, only this time from both sides. The windows rattled, the doors bent in, and there was a noise outside that was not the wind. It sounded more like heavy breathing, and Keith reached for the shotgun he kept behind the seat.

"You see somethin'?"

"Just snow."

"Then—"

"I *heard* something."

The vehicle rocked again, hit from behind. Keith spun, saw nothing, listened. He heard the sound of breathing again and, with an angry huff, pushed open his door.

"Where ya goin'?"

"To put a hole in whatever's doing this," he said as he jumped into the snowstorm.

The breathing was coming from behind, and Keith sidled back along the cab, looking toward the plain.

What he saw caused him to stop abruptly.

Moving back and forth, over a stretch reaching from the rear of the truck to roughly two hundred yards beyond, were air pockets where the snow wasn't blowing. The blizzard swept around them and over them, as though solid objects were there, but never through them.

Keith looked on with amazement, then inched toward them.

It was incredible, but in shape and size, the pockets looked almost like horses. Now that he thought about it, the breathing sounded like horses as well. One of the air pockets shifted toward the back of the pickup and it rattled again. They *kicked* like horses, too.

"Keith?"

Something occurred to the surveyor just then. He ran back to the cab, reached in, and shut off the engine. His companion looked at him.

"What're you doin'?"

"Trying to stop the knocks. Come out and take a look at this."

Ward did as his boss said, holding his collar shut with one hand as he shielded his eyes with the other.

"What the hell are they?" he asked. "They look like giant bubble-shapes."

"Remember, when we were kids, the animals that starved in the mountains during the winter?"

"Sure. Then we'd come out in the spring to find their bones. So?"

"Do you remember what happened that time with the elk?"

"The one we thought was walking after us when we took its skull?" Ward gazed from the shapes to Keith. "Wait a minute. You can't be serious. What's out there is some kind of wind, not dead animals."

"Herds of wild horses used to get trapped in the mountains by landslides. Who says these aren't them?"

"Because you're talkin' ghosts, Keith."

"That elk seemed real enough that time."

"We were kids—"

"Does that make it any less real?"

Both men regarded the shapes.

"Suppose these are spirits of some kind," Keith said, "travelling with the storm. They felt the car's warmth, tried to get to it. They acted on instinct, just like any animal would."

"Ghost animals roaming the plains of America," Ward said. "An' I thought *The Exorcist* was somethin' pretty weird."

The shapes had begun to move away, back toward the hills. Keith and Ward watched as they vanished into the storm, then the men returned to the pickup and started it, driving off with no further knocks.

Thereafter, whether together or alone, driving the lonely roads or sitting at home or even joining friends for a burger at the charcoal diner in Basalt, each man would wonder whether that was only the wind or a branch which was moving against the window, or whether it was a lost soul that had lost its way—permanently.

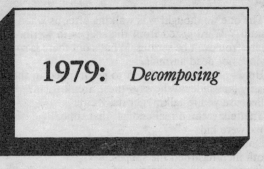

# 1979: *Decomposing*

Priscilla and Franklin Moran came from Florida to the northeast in order for Franklin to continue his music history studies at Yale. They rented an old, rundown home in Fairfield, Connecticut, because it was all they could afford that was relatively close to the school; they had to make do on Priscilla's income from teaching violin and piano, and from the money Franklin brought in working nights at a local record store.

Priscilla had also felt an inexplicable contentedness when the agent showed them the place, something the young woman attributed to the small, neat garden out back.

In what little spare time she had, usually while Franklin was gone at night, Priscilla wrote songs, hoping to be able to sell something to a pop singer or an advertising agency—anything.

The old Knabe piano they'd brought with them from Florida was in the den. The house was small, with just one bedroom, a moldy basement they didn't bother to use, and a small kitchen and dining area. The den, at least, had French doors which looked out onto the garden. At night, Priscilla liked to open them and let the cool fall air into the room.

While she was working at the keyboard one night, Priscilla became aware of soft, harplike music playing somewhere near. She sat on the bench and listened. With some surprise, she realized that the music was coming from the back of the piano, as though someone were gently plucking the strings.

Then there was nothing, but the memory of the bittersweet, polytonal melody.

Deciding that she'd been working too hard, Priscilla went to bed. The following night, while playing back a jingle she'd composed, the young woman suddenly found herself playing not her own composition, but the air she'd heard the night before.

She stopped and rubbed her hands together, then heard the rustling of papers from somewhere behind her. She turned and it stopped, replaced by a man's voice softly humming the strange melody. Then, it too was silent.

Frightened, Priscilla rose from the stool and looked around the den. No one was there. The garden, too, was empty, and she shut the doors. She sat back down at the piano and looked at her music: only it wasn't her music. The sheets were yellowing, the notes were faded, and the title, "The General's Dilemma," was written in a hand not her own.

As she leaned closer to see the composer's name, the man's voice came again, from the kitchen. It was still humming the song. Following it, she found the kitchen empty and the voice now coming from behind the door which led to the basement.

Franklin came home then, and Priscilla went to greet him. All through the night, however, she was haunted by the music, and heard the man humming the song over and over in her head, despite her best efforts to ignore it. She slept little, and was hardly ready to give her lessons that day.

But exhaustion wasn't the worst part. When the first pupil, a five-year-old girl, sat down, she played the music Priscilla had heard the night before.

The teacher stared at the girl as her little hands worked

the keys. The music in front of her was the faded music the woman had seen the night before.

Somehow, Priscilla managed to get through the lesson. She used the half-hour break until the next student to wash her face and make some tea. The song continued to play relentlessly through her head, and then, once again, she heard the voice of a man humming it from downstairs.

She went to the basement door and stood listening, then opened it and shouted down. The man continued singing. She threatened to call the police. Still he sang.

Priscilla's next student arrived then, and, like those that followed, every other song they seemed to play was that one mysterious melody. Somehow, the teacher got through the day. When the last student had left, Priscilla lay in bed, turned on a cassette player, and listened to Wagner, trying to blot out the song.

The same, odd song came from the small speaker.

Priscilla shut it off, but it continued to play, joined by the piano and then by the man's voice, once again coming from downstairs. Unable to stand it any longer, she ran down to the kitchen, grabbed a butcher knife, snapped on the basement light, and walked slowly down the rickety wooden steps.

The music grew louder as she reached the small, damp basement. She looked around in the light of the bare bulb: there were only old, crumbling cartons lying about, and a few crates covered with a film of green mold.

The piano was ringing, the man humming loudly, and Priscilla clutched at her ears. The music seemed to be coming from the corner of the room, and she stumbled ahead.

She looked down at the crates, and in one was a fat bundle of handwritten music. She bent: the one on top was the same she'd seen on her piano. The music was deafening now and, pushing her knife under the twine which bound them, Priscilla reached for the music. Grabbing a handful, she stood and saw the man who was humming. She recognized him, but truly and sincerely didn't want to. Tearing at the sheets, she ripped them up and tossed them aside. All the while, the music and the figure of the man grew more faint.

When she was finished, and could still hear the tune being

played on the piano, she went back and shredded the compositions further.

When the melody was finally gone, Priscilla lay forward, panting. Physically and emotionally drained, she soon fell asleep.

When Franklin came home, he found his wife lying on the cement floor, surrounded by the destroyed music. She muttered that music wouldn't leave her, that the composer himself had come to see her, that he didn't want his music to rot in a basement, but that he was making her crazy. It was obvious to Franklin that his poor wife had been working much too hard, and after helping her up to bed and seeing that she was all right, he went back downstairs.

He began sifting through the tatters. The music was irreparably destroyed, though on one scrap he could still make out the composer's name: Ives.

Franklin swore.

Charles Edward Ives. An innovative American composer, he was largely ignored during his life and was only now being rediscovered. Ives was taught by Horatio Parker of Yale; this may have been where the composer lived for a time, or where he had stored his music for whatever reason: original, hitherto unknown compositions, which Priscilla had destroyed.

For a while, Priscilla would hear the music in dreams, though she resisted the urge to write it down, to give it a fresh hold over her. And in time the dreams faded too, as the composer finally seemed to accept that this was one work destined never to be heard again in this world.

# 1979: The Specters of Norse America

Dr. Edgar Hodes was among the many archaeologists who had a problem with the Vikings: unlike some of his colleagues, the college professor and expert in dead and ancient languages wasn't convinced the Norsemen ever made it to the North American continent. A trip to view a possible eleventh-century relic discovered 171 years before on Manana Island in Maine was supposed to persuade him that he was wrong.

Manana is a small, wind-lashed nub of rock near the larger Monhegan Island, which lies twelve miles southeast of the mainland. Boating out on a summer morning with his wife Catherine, a former student, the elderly scholar made his way to the small pool above which the inscription can be found, markings which cover an area a half-foot tall and two feet wide.

Catherine touched them. Her husband simply stared, monumentally unimpressed.

The inscription consisted of shapes like *X*'s and *V*'s carved in the stone. They were probably random, as others had suggested, the result of erosion. So much for the imaginative translation made by old Olaf Strandwold: "I, Veigle, lay seven years, 1031."

Returning to the shore, Dr. Hodes and his wife sat on rocks overlooking the sea and broke out their bag lunch, the archaeologist muttering in disgust.

"The revisionists," he complained. "Always making work for us. The Indians and the Europeans were the only ones on the continent. Period."

Catherine laughed. "What was it Dr. Fell came up with?"

"Oh, that was a good one! He said that the Phoenicians were here, trading with the Indians centuries earlier! Translated these bloody damn markings as 'Phoenician long ships, cargo landing quay.' What nonsense. They're just random markings, no more."

The couple sat in silence while Dr. Hodes contemplated the sea. To imagine that any people would have come here and left was absurd. Colonies would have been attempted. Some would have been successful. A Viking or Phoenician presence would have been discernible in other ways apart from those absurd markings. Something like the eleventh century farm from Gjáskógar, Iceland, or the one in Brattahlid, Greenland. There were many ancient farms, buildings, even places of worship and graves found in Greenland.

Looking over at his wife, who had been as silent as he, Dr. Hodes was surprised to see her sitting quite still, her eyes shut.

"Catherine?"

She began swaying slightly. He took her gently and shook her.

"Catherine? Are you all right?"

Her eyes still shut, she climbed from the boulder and knelt on the rocky beach. Pushing away stones, she used her finger to make linear markings in the small patch of exposed sand.

Standing behind her, her husband watched with a mixture of concern and curiosity.

"I am still here," he read as she wrote. His brow furrowed. "*Who* is still here? Catherine, what is this?"

She turned and spoke to him, her eyes still shut.

"The sailing ship," she said, not in English but in a dialect of West Norse, the language of the overseas colonies. "A storm—smashed, it was. Pine and oak . . . not equal to stone. The waves, furious."

Dr. Hodes knew that Catherine wasn't the kind of person to play a trick like this, and in any case she didn't know the ancient Viking tongue. Something weird was happening, and he decided to go along with it.

"You were shipwrecked?"

"Yes."

"How many were you?"

"There were twenty-two. And animals . . . pigs . . . sheep . . . cattle."

"You came from *Ísland?*" he asked, using the appropriate name for Iceland.

"Yes."

"How . . . how long did you live here?"

Catherine replied, "Seven years."

"And your name?" Dr. Hodes asked.

"I am Veigle."

Now Dr. Hodes shook her harder. "Catherine! Wake up!"

"I am Veigle."

The voice was different now, deeper. He shook her harder.

"Catherine!"

"The others have all died. The natives no longer help."

He rattled her harder.

". . . seven years . . ."

*"Catherine!"*

She stopped speaking; her eyes opened slowly; she looked around.

"Edgar?"

"Catherine, do you have any idea what just happened?"

"I do. I *saw* him in my mind, a frail man using a hammer and chisel to carve the runes. Edgar, it wasn't a dream. There *was* someone."

Dr. Hodes wasn't convinced. He wasn't sure he could explain what happened, but he didn't believe that they'd been visited by a ghost.

Leaving the rest of his lunch, he decided to go back to the inscription. Catherine, after all, had been the one who touched the markings.

Crouching and placing his hands on the stone, Dr. Hodes felt nothing strange, neither saw nor heard anything unusual. Until he and his wife returned to the beach.

The seas were suddenly unruly, the surf pounding and spray showering down on him. And the island seemed subtly changed, the rocks in different places, some a little larger.

He turned to remark about it to Catherine, but she was gone. He was alone on the beach, and in clothes that were not his, but the torn raiment of a Norseman. He looked down at his hands, which were callused and rough, hands not his own. He spoke, and neither the voice nor the tongue was his either.

He heard his wife calling to him, and as she did so the image seemed to shift, the beach returning to the way it was, his clothing and hands and voice once more his own.

The remnant, here, was not a farm or a church or a grave. It was the spirit of a Viking explorer himself, using the last mortal object he had touched to convey one final message:

That scholars do not always understand reality. That colonization is as much a result of luck as determination. That the settler *had* been there, and while there were no cities or descendants, a part of him *would* be there, always.

(Note: Dr. Hodes and his wife are the only people who have experienced a haunting on the island. There are those who maintain that it was simply a revolt of the archaeologist's subconscious against his own stubborn refusal to accept the evidence of the markings. However, that doesn't explain what Catherine did and saw. As Dr. Hodes has commented, "A Viking's spirit is a far more credible thing to find there, I think, than a Phoenician's.")

American history buff Kevin Dartmouth loved the plains more than the sea from which he'd earned his livelihood. After a lifetime spent renting boats to tourists in Florida, the widower retired to a small, isolated house in Montana, not far from the Custer Battlefield National Monument. He would spend hours there each week, walking the park and imagining how things were a century before, when the thirty-six-year-old officer led the men of the Seventh Cavalry to their death against a far superior force of Sioux and Cheyenne. He knew many of the 260 fallen soldiers by name, and often talked to them as he walked.

One day in August, however, he was unable to make his customary trip to the park. Early in the morning he first felt the pain, an ache in his side which woke him shortly after dawn and grew in severity throughout the day. He took painkillers, but none of them got rid of the hurt for long, the agony knifing into his right hip until he could no longer walk. By the time he decided to phone the hospital, it hurt just to move at all, so he just lay on the bed, riding the waves of pain, crunching down aspirin, trying not to scream as he prayed for whatever it was to go away.

Early in the evening, Dartmouth began to feel two distinct pains in his chest as well. Only these weren't like the others: they burned inside as well as out, and when he looked at his chest, he saw that his skin was a dark red.

Dartmouth had had a mild heart attack once, and this was nothing like it. He couldn't understand what was wrong.

As if the pain wasn't agonizing enough, by early evening it was clearly affecting his mind. He heard muted cracks, and sounds like the owls he sometimes heard at night, and distant shouts. He smelled smoke and the unmistakable odor of damp soil.

Worse, the few times he managed to open his eyes, he didn't see his dark bedroom, but a darkening sky, like dusk, with blurred images moving past in all directions.

A small, lucid corner of his mind told him he had to be hallucinating. But that didn't make anything he was feeling or sensing go away.

He managed to fall asleep after taking three aspirin late at night; he was awakened some time later not by pain, but by the feeling that he wasn't alone.

He looked around. Above him, again, was the gray sky. He thought he heard the wind blowing, and he smelled more than smoke and mud. His nostrils were full of the scent of blood, sweat, and excrement.

He heard nothing, but felt someone moving by his side. He looked back, and saw the familiar sight of Last Stand Hill, the final position of Lt. Col. Custer. Incredibly, it looked as it must have on that fateful day in 1876. There were bodies upon it, some soldiers, some Indians. The soldiers were naked, and other Indians were moving among them, using the butts of rifles to club the men who were still alive.

Off to the right, higher on the hill, Dartmouth saw two Indians sitting on horseback, looking down, motioning this way and that. One had long, black hair blowing in the wind, the other had braided hair; both men wore feathers and held decorated shields. Their quivers were empty.

One of them pointed toward Dartmouth. The elderly man heard footsteps on the soggy earth, looked in front of him just as a brave approached, barechested and covered with blood. The Indian was holding a hatchet. With a cry of rage, he raised it above his shoulder and brought it down on the top of Dartmouth's head; an excruciating jolt shot through him, down to his feet, and a moment later he lost consciousness.

Then he was awake again, and felt no pain. Nor was he on the battlefield. He was lying on his bed, in his room, light pouring through the window. Except for being drained by his ordeal, he was well. Mustering his strength, he rose slowly, walked to the window and looked outside. He stood there a long time, trying to understand what had happened.

There was no logical explanation, other than that he'd been driven temporarily mad by pain. Whatever had brought on the severe aches—food poisoning or a flu, perhaps—had caused him to imagine that he'd been on the Custer battlefield.

Walking outside, he sucked in the invigorating morning air, then came in to have some food.

He switched on the radio and listened, with horror, as he heard that a fire had ravaged the Custer memorial. Apparently caused by a discarded cigarette, it had cut through 600 acres of the 760-acre field as the Indians had sliced through the Seventh Cavalry: quickly and decisively. When the inferno was finally extinguished, all that remained was charred ground, the terrain stripped of all foliage.

Though he was still drained, Dartmouth dressed quickly and drove over.

Instead of greenery, the plains were once again a vista of death. Dartmouth stood near Last Stand Hill with tears in his eyes. He felt as though the memory of innumerable dear friends had been desecrated. Others walking the grounds had grave expressions, obviously feeling similar emotions.

For years afterward, Dartmouth believed that he had somehow felt the fire and was responding to it. Then he learned something which led him to believe that what he had experienced was far more, that the fire had awakened something more profound in the soil of the battlefield.

Taking advantage of the fire, the National Park Service

hired archaeologists to comb the terrain for artifacts and, using computers to plot the location of everything recovered, to try to chart the course of battle. The undertaking was successful, the four thousand items providing the team with the chance to recreate the battle with remarkable accuracy.

However, of everything they recovered, the most interesting and tragic was the hitherto undiscovered skeleton of a young soldier who had died that day, killed by a combination of two gunshots to the chest, a hatchet wound in his right side, and a crushed skull.

The injuries were identical to the pains Dartmouth had suffered during his own ordeal.

Dartmouth reluctantly told his story to a reporter after the skeleton had been found. He knew it sounded incredible, but he believed that somehow, the fire had disturbed the spirit of the youthful cavalryman, and his death throes were somehow visited upon Dartmouth—probably because he had trod the ground so often, communing with the dead.

The editor wanted the story written as if Dartmouth were a crackpot. The reporter didn't believe he was. It never ran.

Dartmouth continued to walk the battlefield several times a week. And though he never met any other ghosts of the Little Bighorn, he felt more than ever that they were there, reliving the pain and glory that is so much a part of life, and, it seemed, of death.

# 1985: *Missing Him*

Nineteen-year-old Janet Caster, an aspiring actress, read about the tryouts in the newspaper. A big Manhattan video store was looking for someone to put on a gorilla suit and play King Kong for a week, romping outside and roaring at tourists. It would be a fun job, with high visibility and a certain spot on the evening news. She wanted it.

The auditions were the following morning. There wasn't much time to prepare.

At first, she took a train to the Bronx Zoo to watch an ape, to see exactly how it moved. What it did, unfortunately, was just sit there. She decided, instead, to try to get into King Kong's head. She knew she could only do that at the Empire State Building itself where the epic movie had taken place. Taking the subway downtown, she bought a banana at a stand across the street and went up.

The observation area on the eighty-sixth floor was packed with mid-summer tourists. People milled about the souvenir area, walking along the high fences of the outdoor promenade, peering through the big metal binoculars, and even dropping paper over the side to watch it flutter away.

She walked slowly around the four sides of the deck, trying to put herself in the mind of a fifty-foot-tall gorilla.

She stopped and put her hands on the top of the chest-high wall, running her fingers along it. Then clutching at it. She was trying to imagine what it would be like to hold on up here, to have the city at your feet, limbs tired from the climb.

The warm breeze suddenly grew chill, raising goosebumps along her arms. Something seemed wrong; she felt slightly light-headed.

Janet turned to go in, saw that a woman had stepped up beside her. She looked odd, dressed like someone from a fifties television show, right down to the white gloves and pearl necklace. However, she wasn't quite picture-perfect: the little suit jacket she wore looked rumpled, she had on no shoes, and her nylon stockings were ripped. And though it might have been the bright red lipstick she was wearing, her skin looked incredibly pale. Or maybe she just didn't like heights.

The woman was leaning toward the thick metal bars of the fence and looking over the side.

"My man died in the war," she said in a soft voice.

"Oh. I'm, uh, sorry."

Janet didn't know what to make of the woman, or what else to say. She started away and hoped that would be that.

"We knew each other since we were children," the woman said. Janet stopped. "We were to be married when he came home, but he died in Hannover."

"Like I said, I'm sorry."

The woman looked off at the sky. "I feel empty. I can't even cry any more. I've been crying for two years. I decided to come here—" She was smiling faintly. "Here was where he stole his first kiss from me."

*Stole a kiss?* This gal really *was* in the fifties. Janet decided to slip away.

However, before Janet had entirely turned away, the woman got up on the wall, grabbed the fence, and somehow managed to go *through* the links and fling herself forward, arms and legs spread wide. Janet screamed—

And saw people stop and stare at her.

She pressed her face to the fence and looked over the side. There was no one falling, and no one had hit the ground. At least, a crowd hadn't gathered.

She turned and leaned against the wall.

"Are you all right?" a young man with a Greek accent asked.

"Yeah, fine thanks," she said. "Must be the thin air up here or something." She went inside and sat down in the ladies' room, wondering if maybe she hadn't done a little too much running around that day.

She splashed water on her face, and as she did so, the woman stepped up to the sink next to her.

Janet tried to act cool, but she was shaking.

The woman stood there, staring into a mirror.

"You want to tell me how you did that?" Janet asked.

The woman didn't answer.

"The trick with the fence," she said angrily. "How'd you do it?"

"My man died in the war," she said in the same soft voice as before.

Janet felt afraid.

"We knew each other since we were children. We were to be married when he came home, but he died in Hannover."

Janet hurried from the washroom and stood in the souvenir area. She bought a soda, gulped it down, then got in line at the elevator.

When the doors opened, and a crowd of people came out, the strange woman was among them. No one paid her any particular attention.

Janet tugged the sleeve of an elderly woman in front of her.

"Do you see that woman over there with gloves and a pearl necklace?"

The woman looked at where she was pointing, then turned and scowled at Janet.

"I take it that's a 'no,'" Janet said sheepishly.

So the woman *wasn't* real. That hardly came as a surprise, but Janet didn't understand how it could be. Why was she hallucinating? Unless this was some kind of organized trick, like that show she'd heard about—*Candid Camera*.

She took the elevator down, bought some gum in the lobby, then walked onto West Thirty-Third Street. She stood there, her mouth hanging open at what she saw.

An old-time sedan was parked on the street. Its roof was caved in, but everyone was ignoring it.

The woman Janet had seen jump was lying on top of it. She was quite dead, though she was wearing the same peaceful look she had on the observation deck.

Janet turned her back on the car and walked away.

The following day, after trying out for Kong (and losing to a burly bouncer) Janet returned to the Empire State Building. The car was gone, and, walking around inside, she found an old security guard and asked if people had ever jumped off the building. He told her that before the fence was put up, people took their lives that way once in a while. When she asked, he said that he did remember one young woman who'd leapt back in 1947.

"Pretty thing," he said. "Landed on top of a car out there—crushed the darn thing right in. They never did figure out why a woman like that would take her life."

Janet knew but didn't bother to tell him. She just thanked him and went back outside.

A ghost. She'd been talking to the ghost of someone who'd jumped off the building. It had probably happened because of the way she tried to get into King Kong by touching the building so intently. She'd done what she read that people do in séances: picked up the vibrations of the dead.

Either that, or she'd spent too much time dwelling on a fictional monster. Or else it had been one hell of an unripe banana she'd eaten.

In any case, she freaked when she got back to her apartment, staying in bed for two solid days with the lights on. She hasn't been back to the skyscraper, or eaten bananas, since.

(The ghosts of suicide victims have occasionally been seen in the skyscraper, usually at night. Likewise, victims of the crash of a B-17 bomber, which plowed into the side of the building during a foggy night in 1948, have been encountered.)

# 1986: A Worm in the Apple

Mart Abernathy, a shopping mall security guard in Minneapolis, bought the computer cheap.

It was a used Apple III, a model discontinued by the manufacturer, but it was all he could afford. It still worked, and the salesperson said she could get replacement parts if necessary. It would be a machine his kids could use to become what the woman in the store called "computer literate." The woman sold him a copy of a game and the Apple Writer word processing program at cost.

The three Abernathy children were thrilled to have the machine, and Mart's wife Carole was more than happy to put in extra hours at her job in a bedding store to help cover the cost.

However, no one was quite prepared for the unusual extras the computer brought to their lives.

It began late one night, when a clattering sound filled the small Abernathy home. Mart climbed from bed and went to the dining room, where the computer was kept. The drive was clacking and spinning, though the monitor was off. Mart shut the computer off, and the following morning warned the kids to make certain they turned off the machine when they were finished with it. The kids were sure they had, but Mart insisted that they were wrong.

The next night, Mart checked the computer before going to bed. It was off, yet at the same time as on the previous night, the disk drive began acting up. Mart shut it and planned to take it back the next day to see what was wrong.

No sooner had he climbed back into bed than the drive came on again. He and Carole looked at one another.

"I thought you turned it off."

"I did. Must be a short of some kind."

Mart went back in and yanked out the plug, but the machine didn't shut down. Just the opposite: now the green screen came to life. However, nothing appeared on it.

Mart called Carole down, and they looked at the screen with amazement.

"Someone at the computer store had to have done this," Carole said. "There must be a program of some kind built in."

"It's unplugged."

"Then maybe there're batteries inside. Something. What else could it be?"

Mart didn't know. After a few minutes, it shut down and didn't come on again that night.

The next day, Mart brought the machine back. When he went to pick it up, technician Dave Hovis said that while he couldn't explain what had happened, there was nothing wrong with the computer itself. However, he was intrigued enough to tell Mart that if the machine acted funny again, he should call him, regardless of the hour, and he'd come right over.

That night, the same time as before, the computer and monitor switched themselves on.

Dave hurried over, saw that the drive was whirring, and pulled out the plug. It continued to clatter. He stared at the machine until, just like before, it shut itself down.

Dave sat at the machine, Mart and Carole on either side.

The technician looked again at the plug lying at his feet and shook his head.

"If I hadn't taken the computer apart, I'd say someone was playing games with you. But there's nothing in this machine that doesn't belong there."

Dave booted up Apple Writer. When it was ready, he removed the disk, inserted a formatted blank, and typed in *"Who are you?"*

After a moment, a response of sorts appeared on the machine: *"What are you doing at my keyboard?"*

Dave typed, *"This keyboard belongs to Mart Abernathy."*

*"It does not. It belongs to me."*

*"Who are you?"* Dave repeated.

*"Daniel Cohen."*

Dave sat back while the disk saved the communication. "I'll be damned. This unit was previously owned, wasn't it, Mr. Abernathy?"

Mart nodded.

"Obviously by someone named Daniel Cohen," Dave went on, "who had to be a hell of a genius to be able to put in a program that I can't find, along with something to power it."

"If that's what it is," Carole said, sidling toward the wall. There was a strange look on her face as she looked down at the computer and switched off the light.

There was a whitish light around the unit, more than just the residual glow of the screen.

"What the hell is it?" Mart asked.

"I haven't the foggiest," Dave said, rising quickly and backing away from the keyboard.

The glow seemed to move and shift around the machine like a cloud on a mountainside, though a part of it was always touching the front, by the disk drive.

More words appeared on the screen. *"What are you doing here?"* the computer demanded.

Carole went to the keyboard and typed, *"Are you alive, Mr. Cohen?"*

The question apparently startled the machine as much as it stunned Mart and Dave. They stared at the computer as the disk drive spun—not accessing the disk, which had little on it, but running what sounded to Dave like some kind of diagnostic program.

After nearly three minutes, it stopped. Words appeared.

*"Where am I?"*

*"You're in our home,"* Carole typed.

*"No. It's dark."*

Before Carole could think of anything else to write, data began flashing across the screen. At first, it appeared to be graphics of buildings and architectural designs. But the output quickly degenerated into garbage, row after row of letters and symbols. As it did, the glow began to broaden and dissipate, finally disappearing entirely. When it did, the computer finally shut down.

The next day, Dave and Mart checked the records at the computer store.

The machine had been sold by a Mrs. Ellen Cohen, wife of architect Daniel Cohen, who had died of a heart attack four months before. He had been in his office, at the keyboard, when he died.

The computer hasn't acted up again, though every time they hear the disk drive at work, Mart and Carole listen closely, half expecting to hear the kids call out that there are funny messages on the screen.

(Note: There have been a handful of other microprocessor hauntings, the most notable of which is the ghost of chess buff Maurice Tillet, who inhabits the computer chess game of his old friend Patrick Kelly of Braintree, Massachusetts. However, Tillet's spirit can access the game only when his plaster death mask is near the unit. Like the Abernathys' machine, the computer chess set can be worked by the ghost even if it's unplugged.)

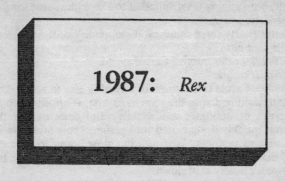

# 1987: *Rex*

Hillary Townsend had an explanation for the bizarre friezes carved into the walls of the Grand Canyon: they were all looking at it the wrong way.

The advertising graphic artist and amateur paleontologist decided to use her vacation time to travel to the Havasupai Canyon near the Grand Canyon, to have a look at the ancient carvings there.

She had obtained permission to explore the canyon in advance, her many noteworthy findings in the fossil field having won her a wide following among professionals. Driving to Arizona from New Mexico, she stopped ninety miles northwest of Flagstaff, at the Grand Canyon's south rim.

With her German shepherd Rex, the forty-year-old reached the isolated spot late in the afternoon. After setting up her small camp, she had just enough time to take a look at the ancient carvings.

Her first impression was that the other researchers were right. The carving, made by human hands, did indeed look like a tyrannosaurus. Common sense, however, told her that that could not be: the last of that breed of dinosaur died out sixty-five million years before any human had set foot on the earth. And for a prehistoric artist to have imagined such a creature was too coincidental. The likeness seemed *too* exact.

But the thing had to have another interpretation. She and the other scientists were seeing what they wanted to see, what they were familiar with. Show it to a rancher or a school teacher or a police officer, and they would see something else. In the morning, she would take a fresh look at the figure, examine it in the context of the entire frieze.

Going back up the path and lighting a fire as the sun began to set, Hillary put a steak in an iron pan, sat back, and gazed at the orange sky.

Rex's ears perked. She looked at him.

"What is it, boy?"

The dog's head came up from his paws, and he gazed along the top of the rim, his head cocking from side to side. Hillary scratched the back of his neck.

"Hear a rabbit? A field mouse?"

He startled her by beginning to whine. Then he backed along the ground, lying low, hesitating, and finally slunk toward her Bronco II and crawled under it. He lay there shaking, refusing to come out even when Hillary tilted the pan toward him and showed him the frying steak.

"Rex! Come on, we've camped out before! You smell something? Another dog? A wolf?"

Alarmed herself, Hillary went to the car and got the .38-caliber Colt revolver she always took on camping excursions and on business trips to New York and L.A.

She bent over and tried to coax the dog out again. Failing, she faced the red skies and walked toward the canyon rim.

There was nothing below. And nothing behind her. She wondered if the dog had sensed an earthquake in the making. She had visions of the frieze wall collapsing, of archaeologists from all over the country whispering her name, ascribing to her the kiss of death.

The smell reached her on the still air. It came from behind

her, rank and oily, and she looked across the darkening flatlands. Rex was still, quieter and meeker than she had ever seen any dog. She thought of dousing the fire, but it was too late. If anything was out there, it already had her pinpointed.

But what *could* be out there? There was no place for a predator to hide.

Then she heard a low rumble, like the guttural sounds of Rex, only deeper. It came from the same direction as the smell, which was stronger now. It was definitely the sound of an animal of some kind.

This was weird. There was nothing out there. She wondered if the sound might actually be from a cat or wolf in the canyon, in a cave, its voice magnified by a series of tunnels.

That seemed plausible, and getting a flashlight from her camp, she began walking ahead, ear cocked toward the sound, trying to find the hole. The rumbling grew louder as she approached, underscored by a gritty sound, like dirt being ground underfoot. For some reason, she thought of a movie she'd seen as a kid, *Forbidden Planet,* where there was a giant, invisible monster on the prowl.

"Sure, Hil. That's what it is."

She wondered if she had accidentally thrown peyote on the fire, and was in the grip of a fantasy.

As she walked, something like heat waves rippled a few hundred yards in front of her—but vertically, not horizontally, reaching to a point some twenty feet off the ground. Behind them, the distant hills blurred, the dark brush ran together, and the sky churned like fire.

The waves grew thicker, and Hillary stopped to watch. They congealed, took on a yellowish hue, spotted with brown patches here and there.

She stopped and stared. Even when the image was fully formed, Hillary didn't believe what she was seeing.

Standing before her was an adult *Tyrannosaurus rex,* its small forelimbs held high, wattles wriggling as it growled. Its jaw was closed, the mouth curving up in the back in what looked like a smile but definitely wasn't. The unctuous smell was overpowering now, but she was too stunned to move. The creature's eyes were upon her as it bent forward slowly, its thick tail straightened and rising behind it as a counterbalance. When its body was nearly parallel to the ground, the enormous beast came forward, shifting heavily from leg to leg, the limbs rising like enormous pistons. Each step brought its feet to the ground with a loud thud which kicked up clouds of dry earth. The claws of its feet were chipped and yellowing, those of the hands somewhat cleaner. When it opened its mouth, she saw that the six-inch teeth were cleaner still.

Then it roared, and she forgot everything, including her name. The deafening sound was accompanied by a blast of fetid wind. Quickly and miraculously, the creature vanished in the same, shifting waves in which it had come. Hillary just stood there; she shrieked when something wet touched her hand.

It was Rex. After nuzzling her, he went ahead, sniffing the ground where the dinosaur had appeared. Then he calmly sashayed back to the campfire and plopped down beside it.

So it wasn't peyote. The dog had seen it too.

Hillary took a pill to help her sleep. In the morning, she walked across the field but didn't see a single footprint or claw mark. She'd seen a dinosaur which hadn't been there.

Hillary spent the day studying the carvings, and waited around until the next night, camera in hand. But the dinosaur didn't reappear. Later, the only explanation she could think of was that a ghostly "radio dial" had been spun. Maybe it was *always* spinning, a spectral "broadcast" from another epoch coming in briefly and then fading. How or why, she never understood, but she did know one thing for sure: she wasn't crazy. Some ancient American had experienced the same vision she had, and had carved on the rock wall what she or he had seen.